History
Columbous.

SPHE 2

Second Year Social, Personal and Health Education

Nodlaig O'Grady
Anne Potts

types of rocks
l believe guys
right make
killkenn sholar
brighter + better

THE EDUCATIONAL COMPANY OF IRELAND

First published 2010
Reprinted September 2010
The Educational Company of Ireland
Ballymount Road
Walkinstown
Dublin 12

A trading unit of the Smurfit Kappa Group
© Nodlaig O'Grady and Anne Potts 2010

Editor: Kate Duffy
Design and layout: Brendan O'Connell
Cover design: One House Communications
Illustrations: Helmut Kollars, Maria Murray, Michael Phillips (Daghda)
Photographs: Alamy, AKG, Getty Images, iStockphoto, Mary Evans Picture Library,
Shutterstock

Acknowledgements
'I Wanna Be Yours', reproduced courtesy of John Cooper Clarke;
'The Rose', by Amanda McBroom, reproduced courtesy of Warner/Chappell;
Water safety images, reproduced courtesy of the Irish Water Safety Association.

Printed in the Republic of Ireland by Colorman Ltd.

1 Think about your first year and how you feel about moving to second year. Then complete these sentences:

1 This time last year I felt _____

2 Now I feel _____

3 A success I remember from last year is _____

4 Something that disappointed me was _____

5 A new skill I learned was _____

6 A challenge that I managed well was _____

7 My favourite subject was _____

8 What I like about being in my class is _____

9 Someone who helped me along the way was _____

10 Someone whom I helped was _____

11 When I got my school report I _____

12 On my report I was delighted with _____

13 On my report I was disappointed with _____

14 If I was back at the beginning of first year again I would _____

_____

15 Something I regret about first year is _____

16 Now that I am in second year I _____

17 I think second year is important for me because _____

_____

2 Now that you have thought about how you feel about being in second year, discuss your thoughts with others. What do you have in common? What are the differences between you? What will help you?

Group Activity

In Activity 1 you identified some things that you would do differently if you were starting off in first year again. Starting second year is an opportunity for new beginnings. Let's look at how you can start anew and explore ways in which you can use your experience of first year to help you through second year.

Activity 2

1. On a page make a PowerPoint presentation aimed at first-year students. Give some advice that you would have found useful in your first year and that will also be helpful now. Design four slides, each advising students on different aspects of school life. Some aspects to include are:

   ☞ What to look forward to
   ☞ Making new friends
   ☞ Who and what can help you with any concerns
   ☞ Your own ideas

   When you have completed your slides present them to the class.
   Keep them safely in your SPHE portfolio.

2. From your PowerPoint slides select three pieces of advice that you will take on board so as to make the most of second year. For each piece of advice write down what will help you to do this.

Advice	What will help me
don't talk in class	don't side beside messers
don't be messing	do your work
don't get in trouble	don't mess
Do your homework properly	Take your h/w down properly

Now that you have named some of the things that will help you make the most of second year, it is important that you set specific goals to ensure your success.

When you have completed Activity 3, you will have learned a framework that you can apply to any situation in your life where you will need to set goals.

Setting goals and targets

1 What would you like to have achieved by this time next year? Jot down as many achievements as you can think of. Think about your personal life, life in school, subjects, sports and extra-curricular activities, hobbies, your friends and family. Let your imagination run wild! Write these things in the circles below. Put the one you would most like to achieve in the centre.

Activity 3

2 Now that you have thought about how you feel about being in second year, discuss with others your thoughts. What do you have in common? What are the differences between you? What will help you?

Differences between goals and wishes

Goal: You have control over your goals! 'I want to improve my fitness.'

Wishes: You cannot control your wishes! 'I wish I was in the musical, but I can't sing.'

> For a wish to become a goal you need a plan. For example, if you cannot sing you could do the props, prompting or make-up for the musical.

3 Look at the words and phrases you have written in the target and divide them into two groups under the headings **Wishes** and **Goals**.

How many of the things that you hope to achieve are actually goals? **Remember a wish becomes a goal when you make a plan!**

Let's look at how you can make a plan to achieve your goals.

You remember Barack Obama's mantra 'Yes, we can!' Well, your mantra is **'Yes, I can!'**

Identify your goal

Make sure your goal is realistic and possible to achieve. Write it down. If your goal is long-term, you may need to break it down into a few short-term goals. These short-term goals are known as targets. Achieving the targets leads to the successful achievement of the overall goal. This will make it more manageable.

Clarify the steps

Clarify the steps you need to take to achieve your goal (or each short-term goal). Write them down. These are the things that you need to do. Set a timeframe for both the short-term and the long-term goals. As you achieve each one, you can mark it off as 'done'. This will keep you motivated too.

Assess the pitfalls

Work at the things that might make achieving your goal difficult. Think of ways to overcome them. If you know what the obstacles are to achieving your goals, you can be better prepared to deal with them.

Negotiate your path

Take action and begin to make the journey towards reaching your goal. Review your progress and if necessary change your plan. Don't forget to reward yourself along the way when you have achieved success.

Pat's goal-setting plan

Here is an example of Pat's goal-setting plan. Read it and then apply the steps to make a plan to achieve a goal of your own in the Learning Log on page 10.

Identify the goal

Pat wants to get a place on the U15 basketball team.

Clarify the steps

To achieve this:

☞ Pat decides to stay for practice two evenings a week after school.

☞ Pat's kit is ready each time.

☞ Pat builds up his physical fitness.

☞ Pat talks to the coach and asks for suggestions.

☞ Pat arranges other time for homework completion.

☞ Pat eats healthily.

Activity 4

Assess pitfalls and find ways to overcome them

Pitfalls	Solutions
Giving up some free time during the week	Make a point of building in free time over the weekend
Finding time to get homework done	Look at adjusting weekly homework schedule
Seeing less of friends	Arrange to meet on Saturday; make new friends at basketball
Watching what I eat	I should be doing this anyway to stay healthy!

Negotiate the path through the steps

Ask advice from a team member

Talk to the coach

Turn up to training

Start to eat more healthily

Do fitness training

Check gear

Review progress at Halloween

Pat has had six weeks training, feels more physically fit and is eating more healthily. He has a positive attitude even if he has not made it onto the team yet. Pat has learned not to blame others and, most importantly, to keep trying to reach his goal.

Learning Log

Select one goal from those you identified in Activity 3, page 5, and apply 'I CAN' to it.

I C A N

Win county U14 C division
train harder and and be more physical
tell trainer to make more training sessions
Do fitness training

▶▶ Group work

During the SPHE class you will be working in a number of different ways, for example on your own, or in pairs, and at other times in small or large groups. In Activity 5, let's learn how to work with others as a team member.

 Activity 5

Group Activity

1. Brainstorm all the words that come to mind when you think of **teamwork**. Write them in the bubble.

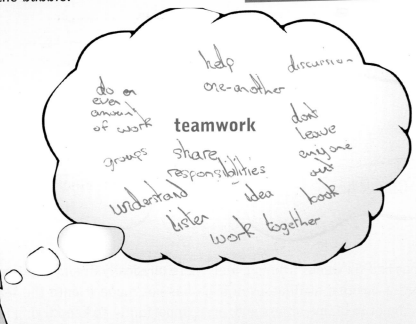

help   discussion
do an   one-another
even
amount   dont
of work   **teamwork**   leave
groups   share   enyone
responsibilities   out
understand   idea   book
listen   work together

2 Think about the words from the brainstorm. Select four that are most important to you and write them below.

From the brainstorm, the four words that represent teamwork to me are:

responsibilities, disscusion, effort, involument.

3 In pairs, share your words and explain why you have chosen them. Together decide which five words mean most to you both and write these down.

Group Activity

Our five words are:

effort, discussion, fun, involument, listen.

4 Work with another pair. The four of you must now come up with a definition of teamwork, using your ten words. Write the definition below.

To ~~us~~ me teamwork is:

people working together to do a project or somthing like that

5 See how this compares with the definitions of others in your class and decide on a class definition. Write it here:

opinion, listen responsibility share and effort.

Ground rules for working as a team or group

Now that you have decided on your definition of teamwork, let's see what ground rules we need so that we can work effectively as a team.

Activity 6

Ground rules

Group Activity

1 Think back to the ground rules that your class drew up last year. Write down the ones you can remember. Add the rules that others can remember and that you may have forgotten, to make a complete list.

Ground rules for our class

1 _____

2 _____

3 _____

4 _____

5 _____

6 _____

New rule _____

_____

2 Look at the rules and answer the following questions:

(a) Which rules do you think worked well?

_____

(b) Which rules did not work so well?

_____

(c) Why was this?

_____

(d) What could you change to make the rules work better this year?

_____

(e) Is there a rule you would like to add this year? Write this in the Ground rules charter after New rule.

Learning Log

Think about how you worked on your own and with others, and complete the sentences.

1 One thing that I learned about how I work with others in a group is

_____

2 One thing that I would like to improve in the way I work with others is

_____

Family ties

In first year we learned that each family is unique and different and, most importantly, that our family shapes who we are. In Activity 7 we explore the ways in which our relationships and roles in our family change as we grow up. We will use the theme of the family crest to do this.

Activity 7

1 On a separate sheet draw a large crest that you can put in your portfolio. Think about your family when you were in **second class**.

Section 1	Section 2
Section 3	Section 4

☞ **Section 1: Who was in your family?**
Use drawing, writing or a symbol in the crest, to show the people who were in your family at this time.

☞ **Section 2: What they did for the family**
Think about what these family members did, e.g. played, cooked, cared for other family members. Put this information in section 2.

☞ **Section 3: Your own name or a symbol that represents you**
Write your name or nickname, or draw an image that reminds you of yourself at that age.

☞ **Section 4: Your role and how you contributed to your family**
Describe your role in the family and the ways in which you helped your family.

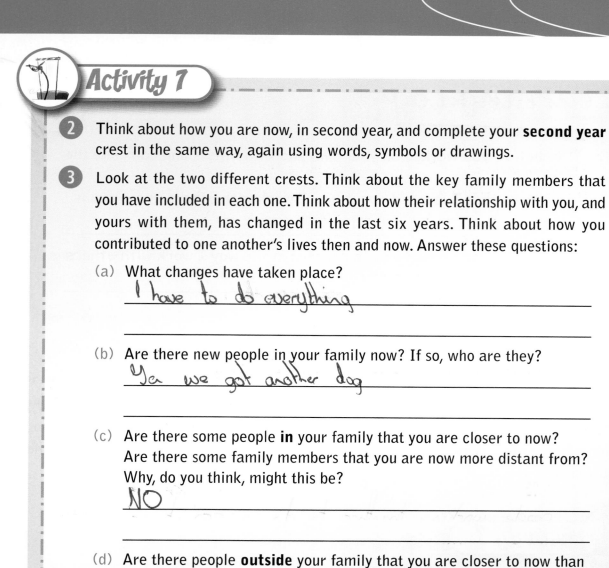

Activity 1

2 Think about how you are now, in second year, and complete your **second year** crest in the same way, again using words, symbols or drawings.

3 Look at the two different crests. Think about the key family members that you have included in each one. Think about how their relationship with you, and yours with them, has changed in the last six years. Think about how you contributed to one another's lives then and now. Answer these questions:

(a) What changes have taken place?

I have to do everything

(b) Are there new people in your family now? If so, who are they?

Ya we got another dog

(c) Are there some people **in** your family that you are closer to now? Are there some family members that you are now more distant from? Why, do you think, might this be?

_NO_

(d) Are there people **outside** your family that you are closer to now than when you were in second class? If so, who are they?

Ya a few people.

Family changes

When you are young, your friends are often people in your family such as brothers, sisters or cousins. As you grow up and become more independent you meet new people and begin to make friends outside your family. This is a normal part of growing up and is an exciting time in your life.

Sometimes, however, friendships break up and new ones are formed and this can be painful. However, you will be able to use the lessons you learn from these experiences throughout your life.

Learning Log

1 Three ways in which I have become more independent of my family in the last five years are:

Have to do all the jobs

Feed the dogs

Make my own lunch

2 One thing that I like about becoming more independent is

Sometimes you get paid for work

3 One thing that I find difficult about becoming more independent is

Fishing

4 Someone who can help me through tough times is _____

because _giving you a chat_

☆ Module Review

Module _____

In this module I learned about

being independant

I think that this will help me _be independant_

I liked _that chapter_

I did not like _the writing_

I would like to learn more about _independance_

This topic links with (another topic or SPHE module, or another subject) _business_

MODULE 2

Self-Management

Introduction

You learned in first year how best to organise yourself at work, at home and in school. Other factors also come into play when it comes to being successful in school. These include having a positive 'can do' attitude, being motivated to work towards achieving your goals, knowing what helps you to learn and developing good study skills. Let's look at how you can be successful this year!

The topics in this module are:

» What motivates me?

» Study skills

 What motivates me?

We will explore what **motivation** means. Let's identify some sources of support and encouragement in our lives.

First let's look at Timmy's holiday.

Activity 1

Timmy's holiday

1 Timmy dreams of a holiday where he can get a lovely tan.

2 Others laugh at his dream.

3 Timmy asks for advice. His friend suggests a plan.

4 Timmy gets a part-time job. He also gets a passport and visits a travel agent.

5 Timmy discovers from friends that booking the holiday on the Internet is cheaper.

6 Every time Timmy saves €50 from his part-time job, he goes to the cinema as a reward.

7 He loses €50 and opens a savings account to keep his money safe.

8 Timmy goes on holiday and meets a cute mouse by the pool where they both get a beautiful tan.

1 What is Timmy's aim?

To save enough money to go on holiday.

2 What are the things that helped him to achieve this aim?

He got a part time job

Motivation

Motivation is the **desire** to achieve a goal, together with the **energy** and **commitment** to work towards that goal. It is an inner feeling that drives you towards achieving a result.

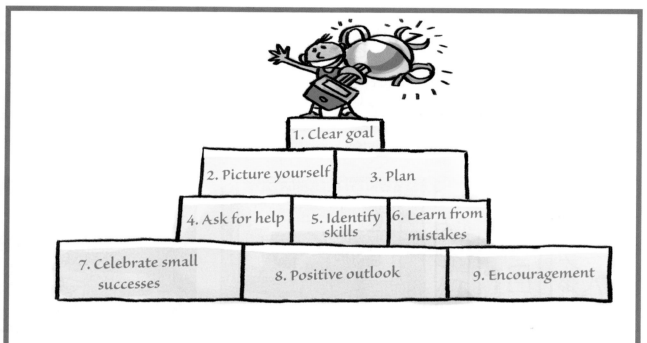

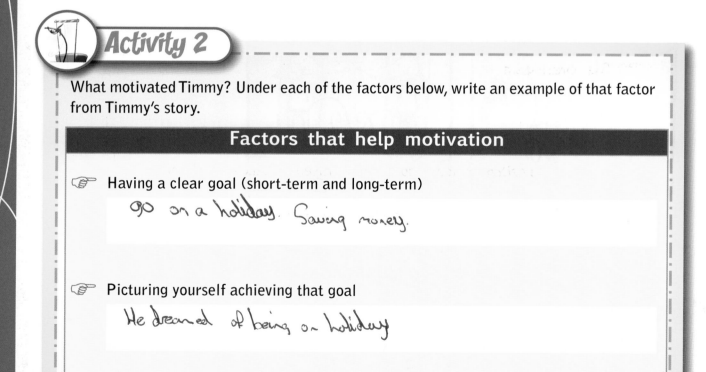

Activity 2

What motivated Timmy? Under each of the factors below, write an example of that factor from Timmy's story.

Factors that help motivation

☞ Having a clear goal (short-term and long-term)

> go on a holiday. Saving money.

☞ Picturing yourself achieving that goal

> He dreamed of being on holiday

Factors that help motivation

☞ Making a plan to help you work towards your goal

get part time job + advice

☞ Being willing to ask for help and support

asked a freind - travel agent

☞ Knowing the people and skills that will help you to reach your goal

Freinds, cheaper on line

☞ Not giving up when things go wrong but learning from your mistakes

when he lost money set up bank account

☞ Celebrating smaller successes and milestones (targets) reached

going to the cinema

☞ Keeping a positive outlook and doing positive self-talk – 'Yes I can!'

when he lost money

☞ Having someone who will encourage you

Freinds

Activity 3

Snakes and ladders

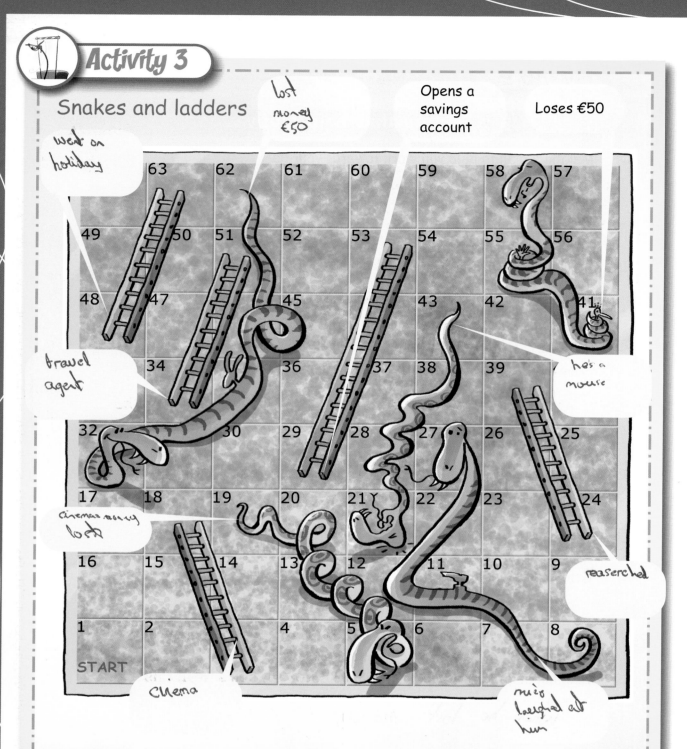

Here is your snakes and ladders board.

1. On each of the ladders write something from Timmy's story that motivated him and kept him going towards his dream. One has been done for you.

2. On each of the snakes write an event from the story which was a setback or an obstacle (barrier) to Timmy following his dream. One has been done for you.

Timmy achieved his dream because he was motivated. Becoming motivated to change something in your life can be difficult. Motivation is affected by what you **think**, what you **do**, how you **feel** and how your **body** is. What you **think** and **do** are the most important of these four, as they affect how you **feel** and how your **body** is. Examine the example in Activity 4.

It's your choice!

James is dropped from the local football team. He can react in one of two ways. Examine the following two outcomes and decide which is the best way for James to respond.

Response A

What James is THINKING	What James is DOING
☞ The coach has favourites ☞ I'm better than others who are on the team ☞ The coach doesn't like me ☞ I'm no good ☞ It's who you know that counts	☞ Complaining about the coach ☞ Blaming himself for not making the team ☞ Taking it out on others: friends, family ☞ Sulking ☞ Giving up training ☞ Overeating or drinking
What James is FEELING	**How James's BODY is**
☞ Angry ☞ Rejected ☞ Resentful ☞ Frustrated ☞ Victimised (picked on) ☞ Useless	☞ Agitated ☞ Hard to sleep ☞ Difficulty concentrating ☞ Stomach in a knot ☞ Red face – boiling!

Activity 4

Response B

<table>
<tr><td>

What James is THINKING

☞ I am slower than some of the others

☞ The coach has nothing against me personally

☞ I will ask the coach what my weak points are and work on them

☞ I will get back on the team

</td><td>

What James is DOING

☞ Doing extra fitness training

☞ Working on his speed

☞ Keeping in contact with the coach

☞ Letting the coach know that he is interested

☞ Watching his diet

</td></tr>
<tr><td>

What James is FEELING

☞ Focused

☞ Involved

☞ Less angry

☞ Happier

</td><td>

How James's BODY is

☞ Relaxed

☞ Fitter

☞ Healthier

☞ Better able to perform

☞ Sleeping properly

</td></tr>
</table>

Important!
Did you notice that if you change what you think and do, other aspects change as well?

1 Which response, A or B, do you think is the best one?

2 What are your reasons for this?

The second one because in this one he is not giving up and he thinks he will get back on the team.

Activity 5

Luca is a second-year student. She wants to do higher-level maths and her class will be divided into higher and ordinary level, based on the Christmas tests.

In September Luca finds out that the maths teacher is someone she doesn't get on too well with. She is afraid that she will not do well enough at Christmas to make the honours class and wonders what she can do.

She has two choices. Below is one of them.

Look again at what Luca is thinking, what she is doing, how she feels and how her body is.

What Luca is THINKING
- ☞ The teacher doesn't like me
- ☞ I'm not going to make the honours class
- ☞ The teacher doesn't want me in her class
- ☞ I hate maths
- ☞ I'm no good at maths

What Luca is DOING
- ☞ Complaining about the teacher
- ☞ Talking about how she has no chance of getting into honours maths
- ☞ Not trying to study maths
- ☞ Blaming the teacher for the situation

What Luca is FEELING
- ☞ Helpless
- ☞ Worried
- ☞ Angry
- ☞ Victimised
- ☞ Hopeless

How Luca's BODY is
- ☞ Tired
- ☞ Anxious
- ☞ Stressed

When you change your attitude, everything else changes as well.

Activity 5

Imagine that Luca decides that she will make the honours class. In the boxes below change what Luca is thinking and doing. Notice how that is going to change the feeling and body sections as well.

What Luca is THINKING
- She will get into honours.

What Luca is DOING
- studying harder than ever

What Luca is FEELING
- Confident
- Hopeful

How Luca's BODY is
- not stressed
- not tired

Learning Log

Think of an example from your own life where what you thought and did were unhelpful. Suggest a better way of dealing with the situation.

Situation:

☞ What I was thinking:

that I was going to get into trouble

☞ What I was doing:

not my homework

☞ What I was feeling:

annoyed because I was going to get into trouble

☞ How my body was:

Anxx

Study skills

In *SPHE 1* you learned how to organise your school timetable and homework. This year we will explore different learning styles. We will discover your preferred learning style and introduce some methods to help you learn efficiently.

Q. Do you have difficulty learning something because of the way it is taught? But if you could teach it to yourself, you would have no problem with it?

A. This is because each of us has a preferred learning style. Knowing your learning style helps in planning how you study.

There are three basic learning styles. Most people have one that describes them better than the other two.

Visual learner	Auditory learner	Tactile/kinesthetic learner

Visual learners learn by watching and reading. They call up images from the past when trying to remember. They picture the way things look.	Auditory learners tend to spell phonetically. They can have trouble reading, because they don't visualise well. These students learn by listening. They remember facts that are presented in the form of a poem, a song or a melody.	Kinesthetic learners learn best through movement and manipulation. They like to find out how things work and are often successful in practical subjects, e.g. carpentry, art or design.

Activity 6

My learning style

1 I think my preferred learning style is

tactile/ kinesthetic learning

2 I think this because

_____

_____

_____

_____

_____

_____

Activity 7

Quick Learning-Style Quiz

Do this quick Learning-Style Quiz to check if you correctly identified your learning style.

Instructions

For each of the nine questions tick √ the answer that is most like you.

1 I remember things best if:

(a) I write them down and read them back to myself ☒

(b) I make lists of the main points and rewrite them repeatedly ☐

(c) I record the information and listen to it ☐

2 I remember:

(a) Faces ☐

(b) Names ☐

(c) Names and faces if I can shake hands ☒

3 I like to learn using:

(a) Lab work and demonstrations ☒

(b) Rhyming chants that I make up ☐

(c) Photographs and diagrams ☐

 **Activity 1**

Quick Learning-Style Quiz

4 When I study I like to:

(a) Sit, walk around and stand some of the time ☐

(b) Use a highlighter to mark the important pieces ☒

(c) Chant the main points to help me memorise them ☐

5 I have trouble remembering information if:

(a) I cannot discuss it in class ☐

(b) I read it and do not talk about it in class ☐

(c) I cannot take notes ☒

6 I study best:

(a) In a group so I can discuss the information with others ☐

(b) On my own in a quiet place ☒

(c) With one other person using role-playing games ☐

7 If I am learning about a new mobile phone or camera, I learn best by:

(a) Using the phone or camera ☒

(b) Reading the instructions ☐

(c) Someone telling me about it ☐

8 When I study for a test it helps me if:

(a) I trace pictures, charts and diagrams with my finger ☐

(b) I read aloud ☐

(c) I organise the information into diagrams, spidergrams and flow-charts ☒

9 Sometimes when I am studying on my own I will:

(a) Act out information ☒

(b) Draw a picture showing a process or an event I need to remember ☐

(c) Create songs or rhymes with my homework ☐

Scoring: (Your teacher will help you score the quiz)

Visual _____ Auditory _____ Tactile/Kinesthetic _____

From this quiz my preferred learning style is

Auditory _____

_____

How well do you know yourself? Is this the same learning style that you identified for yourself in Activity 6 on page 26?

When you know your learning style, you can use it to help you study more efficiently. For example, if you are a visual learner you could use a highlighter to mark the important points in your textbook. This makes the information stand out in a way that appeals to visual learners.

The suggestions in this table may help you to use your preferred learning style to improve the way you study.

Visual learner	Auditory learner	Tactile/kinesthetic learner
☞ Use pictures, charts, maps, graphs ☞ Read books with diagrams ☞ Watch TV programmes ☞ Use computers and film ☞ Write a story and illustrate it ☞ Use colour and highlighter ☞ Take notes in class ☞ Have a clear view of the board and the teacher ☞ Turn the information into flow-charts and brainstorms ☞ Study in a quiet place	☞ Join a class discussion group ☞ Start a study group ☞ Revise by closing the book and saying the material ☞ Read your textbooks aloud ☞ Listen to radio programmes ☞ Turn essay answers into speeches ☞ Use mnemonics to help you remember facts, i.e. use initial letters to remember a list, e.g. HOMES is a reminder of the five great lakes in the USA: Huron, Ontario, Michigan, Erie, Superior	☞ Take frequent study breaks ☞ Move around, pace and stand while studying ☞ Music, without lyrics, may be helpful ☞ Make posters of the information and put them up where you study ☞ Try making models, actually doing the experiment or cooking the dish ☞ Skim through the whole piece before trying to learn it in detail ☞ Use different colours to organise your work ☞ Write or type out the main points

Activity 8

1 In the list on page 28, for your learning style, tick the things you already do while studying and underline those that you will try during the next week.

2 Compare how you study at present with students who have the same learning style as you.

Group Activity

(a) What do you have in common, in how you learn?

_____

_____

(b) What favourite subjects do you share?

_____

_____

Effective study

So let's look at ways to help you remember what you learn at school.

Did you know?
We forget 42 per cent of what we learn in the first 20 minutes! Within 24 hours, if we have not studied the information we learned in class, we will have forgotten 80 per cent of it.

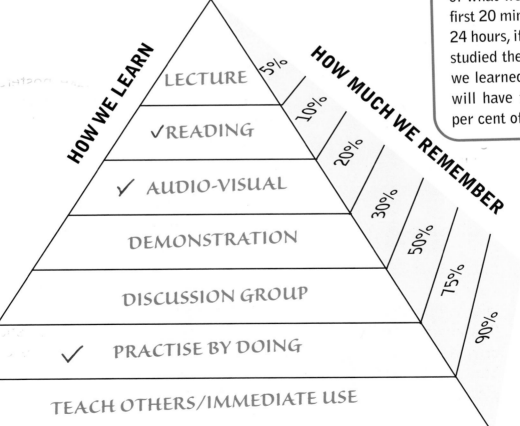

HOW WE LEARN

HOW MUCH WE REMEMBER

LECTURE — 5%

✓ READING — 10%

✓ AUDIO-VISUAL — 20%

DEMONSTRATION — 30%

DISCUSSION GROUP — 50%

✓ PRACTISE BY DOING — 75%

TEACH OTHERS/IMMEDIATE USE — 90%

Learning aids

Summarising and mind maps

Summarising material and making mind maps help you to reduce the amount of material you have to remember. They make you:

☞ Pick out the important points from the material
☞ Link the new material to what you already know
☞ Make it easier to recall it when needed.

Mnemonics, as already explained, means using the initial letters of keywords to help you to remember a list of information.

For example, Richard of York gave battle in vain helps us to remember the correct order of colours in a rainbow: **red**, **orange**, **yellow**, **green**, **blue**, **indigo** and **violet**.

Flash cards contain the essentials, perhaps six main points that would form six paragraphs of an answer. They are created while a student is studying a topic, and then used for revision immediately before an exam. If that particular topic is on the examination paper, the student would immediately write down the six headings and then flesh them out later into a full answer.

Let's look at how you could use these three methods to help you study, remember and revise. The topic we will apply them to is 'The Causes of the Great Famine'.

The Causes of the Great Famine

The Great Famine in Ireland (1845–1849) had a number of interlinked causes.

When people think of the famine, they automatically think of the failure of the potato crop. Indeed, the famine is often called the 'potato famine'. However, although potato blight was the immediate cause of the famine, it is unlikely that its disastrous effects would have been so severe without a number of other factors.

The population had grown to eight million, twice what it is today. Most of these people lived in the western half of the country, where the land was infertile and could not support them. Many of the poor had large families in the hope that some of these children would support them in their old age. Already small, farms were divided up (sub-division) among the sons as they married. This made each farm even smaller and many were too small to support the people living on them.

Farmers, called tenant farmers, did not own the farms they worked on, but rented them from landlords. Many landlords lived in England and did not know what was happening in Ireland. While the famine was going on, much of the food produced in Ireland went to pay the rent for these farms.

The large population depended on the land for food. In the poorest areas, the crop grown most was the potato, as it produced a large amount of food. Growing mostly one crop is called **monoculture**. Potatoes were eaten at every meal.

At the beginning of the famine about one-third of Irish people, mainly in Munster and Connaught, depended almost totally on the potato for food. Any other crops or animals produced on farms were used to pay the rent.

In the mid-nineteenth century the potato crop developed a disease called potato blight. This caused the potatoes to rot in the ground and become inedible. For several years, many of the population had nothing to eat and starved to death.

During the winter of 1846/47, Ireland had some of the coldest and wettest weather on record. This greatly added to the hardship and to the number of deaths. The poorest people had sold their clothing to buy food in the first year and many now froze to death.

First, reread the text, then pick out the main points and use them to make a mind map. Use a highlighter to help with this, as shown below.

The Causes of the Great Famine

The Great Famine in Ireland (1845–1849) had a number of interlinked causes.

When people think of the famine, they automatically think of the failure of the potato crop. Indeed, the famine is often called the 'potato famine'. However, although potato blight was the immediate cause of the famine, it is unlikely that its disastrous effects would have been so severe without a number of other factors.

The population had grown to eight million, twice what it is today. Most of these people lived in the western half of the country, where the land was infertile and could not support them. Many of the poor had large families in the hope that some of these children would support them in their old age. Already small, farms were divided up (sub-division) among the sons as they married. This made each farm even smaller and many were too small to support the people living on them.

Farmers, called tenant farmers, did not own the farms they worked on, but rented them from landlords. Many landlords lived in England and did not know what was happening in Ireland. While the famine was going on, much of the food produced in Ireland went to pay the rent for these farms.

The large population depended on the land for food. In the poorest areas, the crop grown most was the potato, as it produced a large amount of food. Growing mostly one crop is called monoculture. Potatoes were eaten at every meal.

At the beginning of the famine about one-third of Irish people, mainly in Munster and Connaught, depended almost totally on the potato for food. Any other crops or animals produced on farms were used to pay the rent.

In the mid-nineteenth century the potato crop developed a disease called potato blight. This caused the potatoes to rot in the ground and become inedible. For several years, many of the population had nothing to eat and starved to death.

During the winter of 1846/47, Ireland had some of the coldest and wettest weather on record. This greatly added to the hardship and to the number of deaths. The poorest people had sold their clothing to buy food in the first year and many now froze to death.

If you are a **kinesthetic learner**, using highlighter colour (or a different colour for each paragraph) will help you remember the information.

Mind maps

Look at the mind map below. This is what the seven main points would look like. If you are a **visual learner**, making mind maps will help you to remember information.

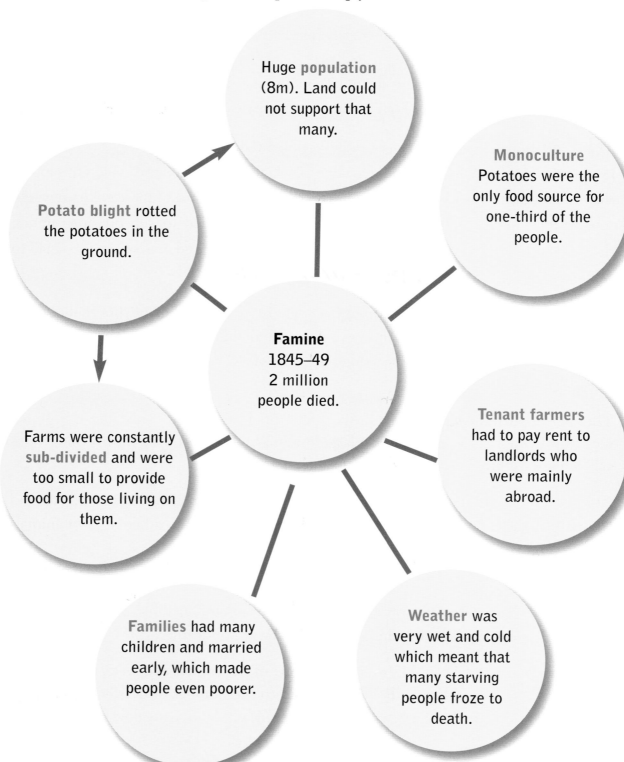

Huge **population** (8m). Land could not support that many.

Monoculture Potatoes were the only food source for one-third of the people.

Potato blight rotted the potatoes in the ground.

Famine 1845–49 2 million people died.

Tenant farmers had to pay rent to landlords who were mainly abroad.

Farms were constantly **sub-divided** and were too small to provide food for those living on them.

Families had many children and married early, which made people even poorer.

Weather was very wet and cold which meant that many starving people froze to death.

Mnemonics

We can make a mnemonic to help us to remember the seven causes of famine – **t**enant farmers, **f**amilies, **s**ub-division, **b**light, **p**opulation, **w**eather and **m**onoculture – by using the first letter of each word as the first letter of a seven-word sentence.

| **T**enant farmers | **F**amilies | **S**ub-division | **B**light | **P**opulation | **W**eather | **M**onoculture |

| **T**he | **F**amine | **S**truck | **B**ecause | **P**otatoes | **W**ent | **M**ouldy |

If you are an **auditory learner**, it will help you to repeat this mnemonic aloud until you can remember it.

Flash cards

A flash card for the causes of the famine might look like this:

Causes of the Famine (1845–49)

1 Population: 8m living mostly on the land.

2 Families: people married early and had more children than they could afford so that they would support them in their old age.

3 Sub-division of farms: there was little education or employment so farms were divided among the sons.

4 Monoculture: because of the numbers that had to be fed one-third of people lived solely on potatoes.

5 Tenant farmers: most people rented land and had to pay rent.

6 Potato blight: wiped out the crop – people had nothing to eat.

7 Weather: very wet, cold weather killed a weakened population.

Looking at flash cards before class or before an exam will keep facts fresh in your mind.

Activity 9

Practice makes perfect

Choose a short piece from one of your textbooks and summarise it. Make a mind map of the main points, invent a good mnemonic and write a flash card for it. Then 'teach' it to your class.

1 How easy or difficult did you find this activity?

very easy

2 Do you think that the other students learned what you were teaching them? (If not, why not?)

No because they wouldn't listin

3 How easy did you find it to learn what the other groups were teaching you?

very easy

4 How does this fit in with the learning style that resulted from completing the Learning-Style Quiz?

good.

Learning Log

Complete the sentence below.

Because my learning style is _____, something I can do

to help me learn is _____

_____

☆ Module Review

Module _____

In this module I learned about

_____

I think that this will help me _____

_____

I liked _____

_____

I did not like _____

_____

I would like to learn more about _____

_____

This topic links with (another topic or SPHE module, or

another subject) _____

_____

MODULE 3

Communication Skills

Introduction

You learned and developed good communication skills in year 1. Hopefully, these have had a positive impact on your friendships and relationships. This year, we will explore further the topics of assertive, aggressive and passive communication and understand that there are occasions in life when it is appropriate to use one style rather than another.

The topic in this module is:

 Assertive communication

 Assertive communication

Last year we learned that there are three main communication styles: passive, assertive and aggressive.

Passive: 'I'm not OK – you're OK'

Passive
I give in to what you want.

Aggressive: 'I'm OK – you're not OK'

Aggressive
You give in to my wants.

Assertive: 'I'm OK – you're OK'

Assertive
We both respect each other's rights, including the right to be different and to be our own person.

Skills needed for assertive communication

Activity 1

Assertiveness means ...

Add any other skills to the diagram that you think are important in being assertive.

Making a complaint

Saying you are sorry

Being able to say 'no'

Asking for help

Giving a compliment

Asking for explanations

Being able to disagree respectfully

Standing up for yourself

Expressing your feelings in a suitable way

Accepting a compliment

Being comfortable with difference

How assertive are you?

Below are eleven statements about assertiveness. Read each sentence and tick whether it is like you or unlike you.

Instructions

Under the 'Score' column, give yourself a rating of 1–4 for each skill (1 = very poor, 2 = poor, 3 = good, 4 = very good).

If there are some groups or people with whom you have difficulty communicating, note this in the third column.

For example, if you can say 'no' to your family, but not to your friends, or you can usually ask for explanations, but not in class, write this information in the space on the right of numbers 3 and 7.

Skill	Score	People who you find difficult
1 Giving a compliment	3 4	Darragh.
2 Accepting a compliment	4 4	Ben
3 Saying 'no'	3 4	John.
4 Expressing my feelings	2 4	Darragh
5 Saying I'm sorry	3 4	Darragh
6 Being comfortable with difference	3 4	Darragh
7 Asking for explanations	2 4	Darragh
8 Asking for help	4 4	Darragh
9 Disagreeing respectfully	3 4	Darragh
10 Making a complaint	2 4	Darragh
11 Standing up for yourself	4 4 3	Darragh.

Activity 2

Scoring
Simply add up the numbers under the score column to get your total.

Less than 15: You need to work on your assertiveness skills or people will take advantage of you. Pick one or two and start with these. When you get more confident you can move on to other skills.

16–27: You are somewhat assertive, but have some work to do in some areas and with some people.

28–37: You seem to be reasonably assertive. Check your answers. Are there some situations that you scored well on? Can you work out why these were better than others? What do you need to work on to improve?

38–44: Well done! You know how to be assertive. Pay particular attention to the next section, on appropriateness, and make sure that you are aware of what is going on for others.

Group Activity

1 Compare your results and discuss the following questions:

(a) Are there some people whom you find it harder to be assertive with than others?

YES

(b) If so, explain why that is.

Because some people are annoying

(c) Are there some assertiveness skills that you are better at than others?

yes

(d) If so, explain why that is.

depends on the person

Importance of assertive communication

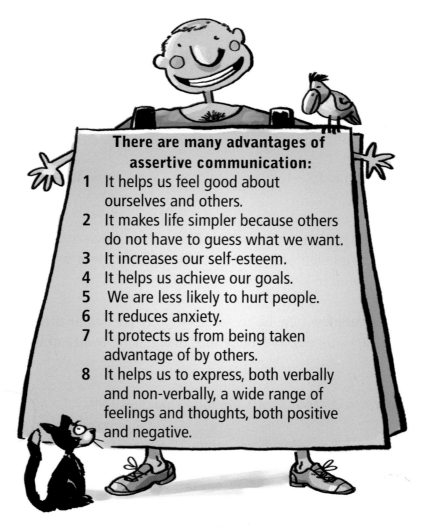

There are many advantages of assertive communication:

1 It helps us feel good about ourselves and others.
2 It makes life simpler because others do not have to guess what we want.
3 It increases our self-esteem.
4 It helps us achieve our goals.
5 We are less likely to hurt people.
6 It reduces anxiety.
7 It protects us from being taken advantage of by others.
8 It helps us to express, both verbally and non-verbally, a wide range of feelings and thoughts, both positive and negative.

Sometimes, there are disadvantages to communicating assertively. Some people may not like this style of communication, or may not approve of the views you express. Our society sometimes thinks expressing oneself assertively is impolite.

Also, having a healthy regard for another person's rights means that **you** won't always get what you want. You may also find out that a viewpoint you held was wrong.

Guidelines for being assertive

☞ Your body should say that you are confident. Take a deep breath, stand up straight, look people in the eye, and relax.

☞ Use a firm but pleasant tone.

☞ Don't presume that the other person is going to be difficult or awkward. Be positive!

☞ Know what you want and say it clearly. Rehearse it first if you think it will help you.

Guidelines for being assertive

☞ Use the 'broken record' technique and repeat and repeat until you believe you have been heard.

☞ Don't forget to listen and ask questions! It's important to understand the other person's point of view as well.

☞ Pick an appropriate time and never make personal or insulting comments.

☞ Try to think win-win: find a compromise so that both your needs are met.

Learning Log

From what I have learned about assertive communication the part I find hardest is

Use a firm but pleasant tone

One thing I can do about this is

talk more clearly

Appropriate assertive communication

Appropriate assertive communication is open and honest and helps people live together in an uncomplicated way. (Appropriate means that it is fitting or suitable for the occasion.) There are times when we have to be sensitive to other people's needs. To do this, we have to change the way we communicate with them.

Remember, while assertiveness is generally the best communication style, there are factors to think about before you respond.

Activity 3

On the following pages are four scenarios that will help you to understand the concept of 'appropriateness'. Read each one and then label the possible responses as 'Assertive', 'Aggressive' or 'Passive'. Then tick the one you think is the best response in the circumstances, i.e. the most appropriate, and say why.

Activity 3

1 A friend of your parents is visiting for the first time. He switched channels on TV to see the News. Your 14-year-old sister had been watching something else.

	Response	Communication style
A	Your sister says, 'Hey baldy, I was watching *The Simpsons.* Turn it back!'	*AGG*
B	Your sister quietly picks up a magazine and reads it.	*PASS*
C	Your sister calmly says, 'Excuse me, would you mind turning back to *The Simpsons*, please?'	*ASS*

The most appropriate response in this situation is A/B/C because

aggresive

_____

Is there a response that you think would be better?

asertive - because she is staying.

_____

2 Your friend's parents have taken you out for your tea. The extremely busy waiter has brought your chips but has forgotten tomato ketchup.

Activity 3

Response	Communication style
A You eat them anyway.	PASS
B You try to catch the waiter's eye and quietly ask for the ketchup.	ASS
C You shout in the direction of the waiter, 'Excuse me, could you bring me tomato ketchup, please?'	AGG

The most appropriate response in this situation is A/B/C because

_____

_____

Is there a response that you think would be better?

_____

_____

③ You are meeting your friend at the cinema. You buy the tickets and wait. And wait. Thirty minutes later, your friend arrives. She explains that on her way out of the drive, her Dad rolled over their puppy and had to take it to the vet.

Response	Communication style
A 'I'm really annoyed. I have been standing here like an eejit for 30 minutes! Why didn't you text?'	
B 'It doesn't matter. I didn't mind waiting.'	
C 'Oh forget it! You're always late anyway.'	

Activity 3

The most appropriate response in this situation is A/B/C because

_____

_____

Is there a response that you think would be better?

_____

_____

4 You are standing on the bus on the way home when you feel somebody's hand taking your mobile phone from your pocket.

	Response	Communication style
A	You shout at the top of your voice, 'Hey, take your hand out of my pocket, you thief!'	
B	You say quietly but firmly, 'Do you mind taking your hand out of my pocket, please?'	
C	'You can have it. I have another one at home.'	

The most appropriate response in this situation is A/B/C because

_____

_____

Is there a response that you think would be better?

_____

_____

Part of growing into adults is learning how to 'read' situations. This means knowing what type of communication style is suitable for different situations.

Personal hygiene crossword

Let's see how much you can remember from your work on the Physical Health module in *SPHE 1*.

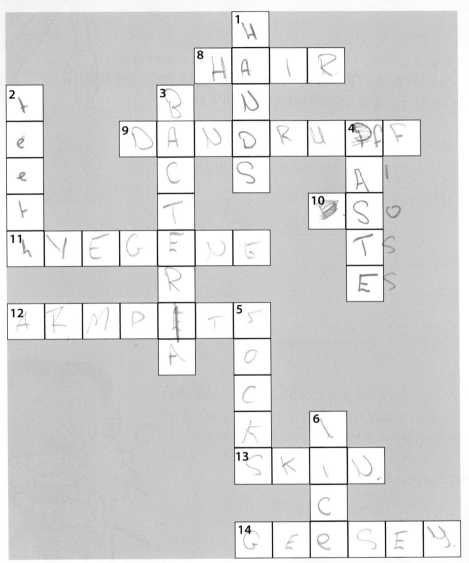

Clues across

8 Shampoo regularly
9 Flakes in the hair
10 Smell from stale sweat
11 Another name for body care
12 Lots of sweat glands here
13 Body surface
14 Oil glands make hair this

Clues down

1 Wash these after using toilet
2 Brush each day
3 Grow in sweat
4 Helps keep your teeth clean
5 Change daily
6 Live in hair

 **Activity 2**

Sometimes teenagers have problems about body care and personal hygiene. In the letters below young people are looking for help with some of these difficulties. Imagine they are writing to you. Read the letters. Discuss what advice would help and write a reply.

Hi Jean
I am 14 and I find that I sweat a lot. I have tried using deodorant every day but think that it just covers up the problem. What else can I do?

Ethel (aged 14 years)

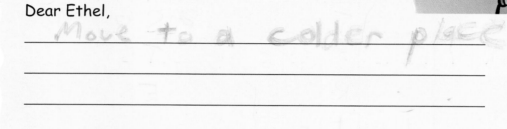

Dear Ethel,

Move to a colder place

Hi Jean
Smelly breath is my problem. I clean my teeth every day but this is not helping. My friend tells me to chew gum to get rid of it but it doesn't work. What causes it and what do you think I should do?

Hal (13 years)

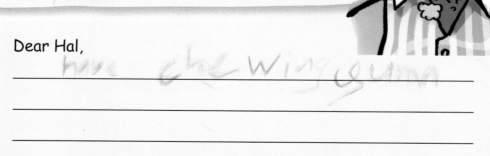

Dear Hal,

have chewing gum

Activity 2

Hi Jean
In the last few months my skin has got loads of pimples and spots. My mam says this is normal at my age but I am embarrassed and when they are really bad I won't go out with my friends.

Marg

Dear Marg,

_____

_____

_____

_____

Hi Jean
I have five brothers and sisters and by the time they have all finished in the bathroom in the mornings, there is not enough hot water for me to have a shower. Sometimes I spray perfume in case I smell bad but I don't like doing this! What can I do?

Flo

Dear Flo,

_____

_____

_____

_____

Body image

Let's explore the links between body image and personal hygiene. What do we mean by 'body image'?

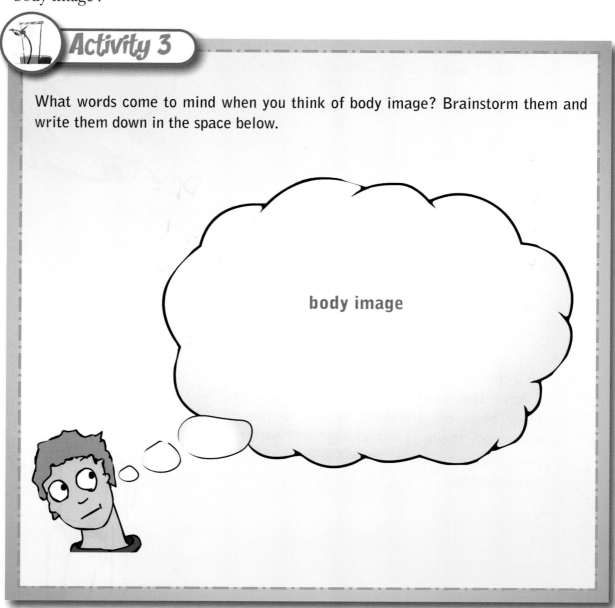

Activity 3

What words come to mind when you think of body image? Brainstorm them and write them down in the space below.

body image

Your 'body image' is the picture you have in your mind of your body, along with your thoughts and feelings about that picture.

Body image can be influenced by several factors, including the media, our peers, friends and family, and our culture. Many of these influences exert pressure on young people to appear in a particular way. You will learn more about this in the Emotional Health module. Having a healthy body image also means that you know how to care for yourself, both physically and emotionally, in a way that enables you to feel good about yourself.

Activity 4

First impressions

Look at the pictures below and then answer the questions.

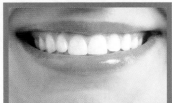

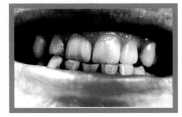

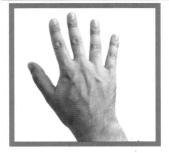

1 What causes someone to look like the photographs on the right?

_____

_____

2 How might others react to them?

_____

_____

3 How might that make them feel?

_____

_____

4 Can you think of other consequences of poor personal hygiene (not being clean)?

_____

_____

Having a positive body image means that you accept and respect your body. Looking after and caring for your body is a key part of developing a healthy body image.

Learning Log

Something I can do that will help me look and feel better is

_____

▶▶ Feeling unwell

As you grow from childhood through adolescence towards adulthood you will learn to take more responsibility for yourself and your health. At this time, your body is changing and growing rapidly. A healthy diet, involvement in physical activity and having enough sleep all contribute to a healthy body. However, in spite of all this there will be times when you will feel unwell and may be ill.

Activity 5

What's your diagnosis?

Let's see how much you know about some common illnesses and their symptoms! (A symptom is an indication or sign of a disease or disorder noticed by the patient.)

Below is a list of some common illnesses and conditions. Look at the table opposite and select the one which best fits the description in column B and write it in column A.

athlete's foot   mumps   warts
excessive sweating   meningitis   acne
eczema   allergies   cold sores   migraines

A: Illness	B: Causes and symptoms
	Changes in hormone activity cause glands to produce excess oils which block pores. Bacteria inside the pore can cause it to become red and inflamed. It is not infectious.
	Occur when your immune system reacts mistakenly to something in the environment that is harmful. Your body produces histamine which causes runny nose, itchy eyes and sneezing.
	A fungus that affects the soles of the feet and between the toes. It thrives in warm, moist areas. The skin becomes red and itchy. It blisters and cracks. This fungus is infectious and spreads in damp areas like swimming pools and gyms.
	Happens during adolescence when glands are active and produce lots of moisture, which lies on the skin. Bacteria can breed here which can result in a smell.
	The skin becomes red and itchy. Sometimes fluid-filled lumps form. Doctors are not sure what causes it. It is not infectious.
	Small blisters form around or inside the mouth or nose. Caused by a virus that most people have lying inactive in their system. When the virus activates these develop. Triggers are sunlight, cold and stress.
	A throbbing pain on one or both sides of the head. Dizziness and nausea are symptoms; lying in a darkened room helps. Prior to the headache some people see flashing lights. Triggers include chocolate, cheese, caffeine, tiredness and stress.
	An infection in the body that travels to the brain where it causes inflammation of the membranes. Caused by bacteria and viruses. Bacterial form more severe than viral. Symptoms include a stiff neck, severe headache, fever, vomiting. It's infectious and requires immediate treatment.
	Caused by a virus spread through saliva. It affects glands throughout the body and especially in the neck, causing them to become swollen and painful. Most children are vaccinated against this disease. It is highly infectious.
	Tiny infections on the skin caused by a virus. Often found as rough bumps on the hands. Pass through physical contact. Take a long time to develop and usually go without treatment. If they persist contact a doctor.

Sometimes when we are ill or feeling unwell it is wise to seek professional help. Your GP (General Practioner) will be an obvious choice, especially if you are ill for more than a day or two, or if you suddenly become sick. However, there are other professionals who can help depending on the nature of the illness or ailment.

 **Activity 6**

Dr Who?

The young people in these pictures have a variety of problems. Look at the list of professionals and suggest the professional that each young person should visit.

> physiotherapist   chiropodist   optician
> GP   dentist   A and E Department

Alan fell awkwardly on his ankle while playing rugby. It seems swollen and is quite painful.

Who should he visit?

_____

Irene has had a toothache for a few days and it is getting worse. She finds it hard to chew her food and often wakes at night in pain.

Who should she visit?

_____

Activity 6

Chris has difficulty seeing the board in class and finds he has to sit closer to the TV to see clearly.

Who should he visit?

____

Louise trimmed her toenail too short and her toe has become red and swollen. She finds it painful to walk.

Who should she visit?

____

Jack fell off his bicycle some weeks ago and is recovering well. His GP has suggested that he needs some additional exercises and suggested that he see someone.

Who does the GP suggest that Jack visits?

____

In Activity 6 you looked at some of the professionals from whom you can seek help if you are unwell. Until you are sixteen years of age you will usually be accompanied by a parent, carer or older adult when visiting a doctor.

However, it is important that you begin to think about what you will need to know and do, when the time comes for you to go to the doctor on your own.

Activity 1

Visiting your doctor

Think about the last time you visited your doctor and jot down your thoughts below.

☞ What did you need to know before you left home?

_____

_____

☞ How did you feel as you went along, in the waiting room, when you went into the surgery, and as you left?

_____

_____

☞ What would have made this visit easier for you?

_____

_____

Tips for your visit to the doctor

☞ Knowing what to tell the doctor is important if he/she is to treat you. Think about this beforehand and write down what is important, in case you forget later.

☞ On the list include your problem, any symptoms and concerns. The doctor's job is to help you, but he/she needs the whole story.

☞ The doctor will put you at ease and help you to explain your problem. Don't worry, doctors have heard it all before!

☞ If you are prescribed some medication ask about it. How long will you be taking it? Are there any side effects?

☞ After your visit, write down what the doctor has advised.

☞ If you have a prescription read the directions carefully.

☞ Make a note of the date and time of any return visit.

Learning Log

You should now be able to complete this sentence:

Some things I can do if I am feeling unwell in the future

☞ _____

☞ _____

☞ _____

⭐ Module Review

Module _____

In this module I learned about

_____

I think that this will help me_____

_____

I liked_____

_____

I did not like_____

_____

I would like to learn more about_____

_____

This topic links with (another topic or SPHE module, or

another subject)_____

_____

MODULE 5

Friendship

Introduction

By now you will have experienced many different kinds of friendship and you will realise that having friends is an important part of your life as a teenager. Friendships can be complicated and at this stage in your life they may be changing a lot. In this module, we will explore the changing nature of friendship. We will also look at the issue of bullying, how you know if you are being bullied and what you can do about it.

The topics in this module are:

- » The changing nature of friendship
- » Understanding, recognising and dealing with bullying

 ## The changing nature of friendship

Friendships can change for a number of reasons. You or your friend might move to live in a different place or change schools. Perhaps you develop other interests, or maybe you just grow apart. Changes like these are part of life and being able to manage them and learn from them is an important part of growing up.

Keeping friendships going takes time and effort. Often, the friends you make as a teenager will be special in that they support you through the ups and downs of adolescence.

 **Activity 1**

Friendship web

When we looked at families on pages 13–15, you pictured yourself when you were in second class. Think about the friends that you had then. Remember that your friends could be relatives, neighbours or people who you know from sports. Maybe you met them on your first day in primary school and stayed friends with them.

1 Choose four people you were friends with in second class and think about how close you were to them. Use a symbol or an initial to represent them and mark it on the diagram below. You are at the centre and the length of the line between you and them will indicate how close you were to them. For example, to show a close friendship use a short line to connect you. Use a longer line for someone you did not know well.

Me

2 Think about the friends you have now and draw a similar diagram.

3 Are there some people who were once closer to you than they are now?
_____ Yes _____

4 If so, are you still friendly with them, even if you are not close friends?
_____ Yes _____

5 Are there others who are closer to you now than before?
_____ Yes _____

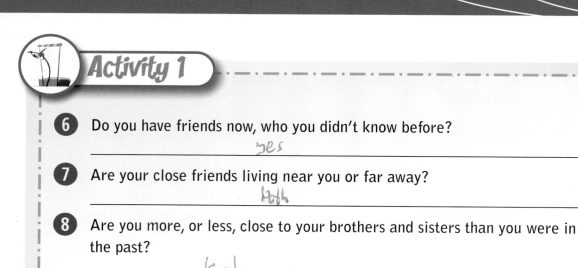

Activity 1

6 Do you have friends now, who you didn't know before?

yes

7 Are your close friends living near you or far away?

Both

8 Are you more, or less, close to your brothers and sisters than you were in the past?

Kinda

9 Why do you think this is?

This is Because Ive become more dependent on them

10 Suggest three reasons why you think your friends have changed.

• older

• cooler

• puperty

Learning Log

Write three things you can do to care for your friendships and nurture them.

1 _____

2 _____

3 _____

Activity 2

The family holiday

Your family is going abroad on holiday and you are allowed bring one friend with you. You have a choice to make.

Activity 2

Here are your friends. Who will you decide to ask along?

Helen
You have become friendly with Helen this year. She is a popular girl in your class and you think that if you invited her, your popularity might increase. Her family is wealthy and last year you went away with them for a long weekend.

Melissa
You have become quite friendly with Melissa in the last year. You knew her slightly from Saturday morning football, before you started secondary school. She loves sport, music and dancing. You know you would have great fun if she came along.

Cora
Cora is a quiet girl who does not have many friends. She is studious and always does well in exams. She has helped you many times with homework. You feel that you should ask her along, to repay her, but are afraid your holiday would not be very exciting if she came.

Georgina
You have known Georgina for years. She was a great friend at primary school. You still do lots of things together. She is loyal and a great listener. Georgina helped you through a tough time in first year when you had problems at home. You know you can depend on her.

Decide who you would ask along and answer the questions below:

1 Who did you decide to ask?

Cora

2 Why did you choose that person?

she's sound

Activity 2

3 How, do you think, might the uninvited friends feel?

Bad

4 How would you explain your choice to the friends you did not ask along?
Do you have to explain to them?

I had to ask cora because she helps me with homework

Your choice will be guided by what you **value** in your friendships. Your values are what you consider to be important. They usually guide our decisions and choices. In the scenarios above these values might be fun, loyalty, popularity, money and respect. As you grow up, your values may change and with those changes your friendships may change also. Sometimes, as in this situation, you may have to make a choice between competing values. This can be difficult.

5 Think about the person who you chose to take on holidays with you. What values guided your choice?

☞ The values that guided my choice were

she helped begin with his homework

6 Three days later you realise that you made the wrong choice and you are feeling upset and cross. You ask a relative for advice.

With a partner role play the discussion you might have. From your role play decide with your partner what the best advice would be and write it on the screen below.

Learning Log

Three things that I value in a friendship are:

1 _____

2 _____

3 _____

Things that I value now that I might not have valued when I was younger are:

☞ _____

☞ _____

☞ _____

▶▶ Understanding, recognising and dealing with bullying

Let's explore different kinds of bullying and identify strategies for dealing with them.

Activity 3

Let's see what we already know about bullying! For each of the following statements say whether you agree, disagree or are unsure.

Statements	Agree	Disagree	Unsure
1 Bullying is just a bit of fun.		✓	
2 Some people take bullying too seriously.	✓		
3 There is no bullying in our school.			✓
4 Bullying can be just a one-off incident.			✓

Activity 3

Statements	Agree	Disagree	Unsure
5 Bullying is deliberately carried out to hurt someone.			
6 There is more bullying among boys than girls.			
7 Girls and boys use different ways of bullying.			
8 Telling someone you are being bullied will make it worse.			
9 Anyone can be bullied.			
10 Anyone can be a bully.			
11 If a person is bullied, he/she should tell someone.			
12 Everyone has a responsibility to stop bullying.			
13 I know what to do in my school if I am bullied.			
14 There are different kinds of bullying.			
15 If I am bullied, I will always know who is doing it.			

There are many different kinds of bullying. Let's explore them a bit more.

Activity 4

Bullying – yes or no?

1 Read the scenarios below. Decide whether or not you think that this is bullying; write yes or no in column 2. (Ignore the last column for the moment.)

Statements	Yes or no	Type of bullying
1 Mary continuously makes snide remarks about Gina's new hair style. Others have started to join in. Gina is embarrassed and upset and Mary knows this.		
2 Peter doesn't like Mike. He meets him in the corridor and deliberately knocks Mike's lunch out of his hand.		
3 Pat, a second year student, tells Jack, who is in first year, that he will 'get him' on the way home if he doesn't hand over his lunch money. Jack has handed over money in the past. So Pat knows that Jack is an easy target.		
4 Joanne bumps into Maura in the corridor and knocks her down. She helps her up and asks if she is OK.		
5 Cora sends cruel, anonymous text messages to Jean. Cora says Jean has BO. Other girls know this. It usually happens when Cora is with a group of friends. Jean sees them sniggering when they see Cora looking at her text messages.		

Statements	Yes or no	Type of bullying
6 Gerry doesn't like Peter. Peter is quite self-confident and this doesn't bother him. Gerry has started to call him names and say Peter is 'gay'. He has also written nasty comments about Peter on notes to other students.		
7 Patricia and Jackie don't want to be friends with Janet. When she walks past, they hold their noses as though she smells.		
8 Tom is a bit of a loner in school and others make fun of him. Paul hides Tom's schoolbag, so Tom gets into trouble in class for not having his homework.		
9 Rose invited Orla to babysit with her, but Orla's mother would not allow her to go. Now Rose posts hurtful comments on Orla's Bebo page.		
10 Steven loves science and continuously gets praise from his teacher for his good work. Now others have started to 'hiss' quietly when this happens. This does not bother Steven at all and he continues to work hard.		

Activity 4

2 Study the descriptions below of the different types of bullying. Read the scenarios again and decide which type of bullying each one is. Write this in column 3 on pages 69–70.

Verbal: Name calling, hurtful comments, teasing, jeering, criticising, spreading rumours, making jokes about someone, abusive phone calls

Physical: Fighting, hitting, damaging others' belongings, spitting, pinching, assault

Relational: Intended to hurt a person's feelings, e.g. excluding others, spreading rumours, humiliating someone, nasty gossip

Written: Graffiti, anonymous notes

Racial bullying: Aimed at those who are different, depending on their race or colour

Cyberbullying: The use of ICT to upset or hurt someone, e.g. text messages, unwelcome emails, using chat rooms and social networking sites, such as Bebo, Facebook

Homophobic bullying: Bullying of young people who are gay or thought to be gay: name-calling, isolation and violence

Intimidation: Playing nasty tricks, threatening gestures, extortion (threatening someone to hand over money or property), nasty phone calls, text messages or emails

Effects of bullying

People can be affected by bullying in different ways. Some of the effects may be short-term, but others may be long-term. Often people who are bullied are afraid to say anything. They sometimes think that if they do tell, things will get worse or others will think that they are weak.

1 Read the scenarios in Activity 4 again. Select one scenario.

Group Activity

(a) Decide what the effects of bullying might be on the person who is the bully.

(b) Decide what the effects of bullying might be on the victim of bullying.

Other people who see bullying are called bystanders. They have a responsibility to do something to stop the bullying, but this can often be difficult.

(c) Decide what the effects of bullying might be on others who see it happening.

Scenario	Effects on bully	Effects on the victim	Effects on bystanders

2 The effects of bullying include:

Class Activity

_____

_____

_____

_____

Activity 6

What can you do if you or another person is bullied?

Brainstorm all the things that you could do if you are being bullied or if you see others being bullied. Think of what you as an individual can do, what your class can do and what your school can do. Write these in the space below. Then divide them into three categories.

what can be
done

1 Things that I can do.

_____

_____

_____

2 Things that bystanders can do.

_____

_____

_____

3 Things that my school can do (remember your school's anti-bullying policy).

_____

_____

_____

The role of bystanders

Ensuring that bullying is stopped is not just the responsibility of the person being bullied. He/she may feel powerless to do anything. Usually others are aware that it is going on; they also have a responsibility. Bystanders can respond to bullying in a number of ways. Here are some:

☞ Walk away and ignore it

☞ Join in and bully, fight, make hurtful comments

☞ Stand on the sideline but encourage the bully by making comments, laughing

☞ Remain passive bystanders and do nothing even though they see it happening

☞ Get support from other bystanders to support the victim

☞ Try to stop the bullying. Talk to the person being bullied. Talk to the bully

☞ Talk to people in authority and seek advice

> **Remember!**
> As a bystander **you** can be part of the problem or part of the solution!

Activity 1

Responding to bullying

Pick one of the scenarios in Activity 4, pages 69–70. Think about ways in which the person being bullied could respond. Here are some suggestions:

☞ Avoid the situation

☞ Use humour

☞ Be assertive

☞ Positive self talk

☞ Ignore it

☞ Tell someone and ask for help from friends or adults

☞ Walk away

☞ Make new friends

☞ Approach each person involved

Write suggestions for the scenario you have chosen.

_____

_____

_____

_____

Remember!
Some approaches suit some situations better than others and suit some people better than others. What is important is that you do something. Work on what suits you. Other areas in SPHE help you to do this.

Learning Log

1 Which parts of the SPHE programme help you deal with bullying?

_____

_____

2 From your school's anti-bullying policy describe how you would respond to bullying in your school.

_____

_____

☆ Module Review

Module _____

In this module I learned about

_____

I think that this will help me_____

_____

I liked_____

_____

I did not like_____

_____

I would like to learn more about_____

_____

This topic links with (another topic or SPHE module, or another subject)_____

_____

MODULE 6

Relationships and Sexuality Education

Introduction

Last year you explored the changes that take place in your lives and your bodies during puberty. This year we will look at how a baby develops from conception to birth. We will also explore the different kinds of relationships in our lives and ways of managing these relationships. We will explore dealing with peer pressure. We will show you how to find help in case you have concerns about any of your relationships.

The topics in this module are:

- » From conception to birth
- » Peer pressure and other influences
- » Managing relationships
- » Respecting myself and others
- » Recognising and expressing feelings and emotions

Before exploring the process of conception and birth, let's see what you can remember about the parts of the female and male reproductive systems, from year 1.

Label the parts marked in the diagrams of the male and female reproductive systems. Use the terms listed below.

cervix   sperm duct   testes
ovaries   scrotum   urethra
vagina   penis   uterus (womb)
fallopian tubes

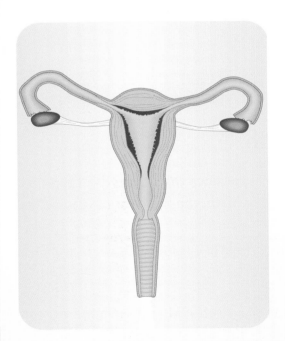

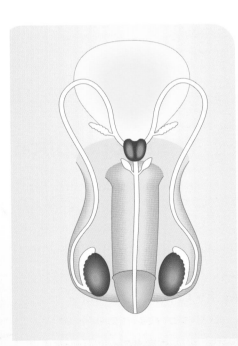

Remember!
It is illegal to have sex under
17 years of age.

 **Activity 2**

In *SPHE 1* you learned that if sexual intercourse has not taken place, the egg dies and is shed from the body. However, if the couple have had sex the story may continue! Now put these sentences in their correct order by numbering them from 1 to 10.

_____ A couple who are committed to one another decide to have a baby.

_____ Sperm swim through the vagina and the uterus into the fallopian tube.

_____ The fertilised egg travels back down to the uterus.

_____ The man places his erect penis in the woman's vagina.

_____ The fertilised egg becomes embedded in the wall of the uterus.

_____ A sperm cell meets an egg in the fallopian tube.

_____ Sperm enter the vagina (ejaculation).

_____ One sperm fuses with the egg (fertilisation) to form a zygote.

_____ During the next nine months, the zygote develops into a baby in the mother's uterus.

_____ The baby is born.

 # From conception to birth

Between fertilisation and death, human beings experience three periods of rapid growth and change. These periods are: from conception to birth, the first year of life and puberty.

Let's look in more detail at what happens from conception to birth.

Weeks 1–12

☞ The fertilised egg becomes embedded in the wall of the uterus about seven days after fertilisation.

☞ First, the brain, the nervous system and the blood circulatory system develop.

☞ 3 weeks: The heart is beating. The eyes, mouth and ears begin to form.

☞ 4 weeks: Arm and leg buds form.

☞ 5 weeks: The sex of the baby develops.

☞ 8 weeks: The baby is three or four inches long.

☞ 12 weeks: The baby is fully formed. It is called a foetus.

Weeks 13–24

☞ The placenta is fully formed, allowing oxygen and food to pass from the mother's blood to the baby.

☞ All the baby's organs are fully formed but need time to develop and mature.

☞ The baby begins to move its arms and legs, fingernails form, hair begins to grow and eyes develop.

☞ 20 weeks: The mother feels the baby's movements.

☞ 24 weeks: The baby can hear the mother's heartbeat and voice.

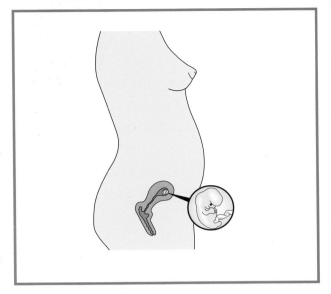

Weeks 25–36

☞ The baby continues to develop and grow, increasing in size and length.

☞ The baby spends time sleeping and is wakeful at other times. Organs such as the lungs mature, so the baby can breathe independently when it is born.

☞ The baby moves into a head-down position, ready for birth.

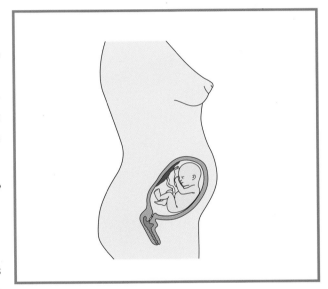

Birth

Scientists are still not quite sure how the process of birth actually begins! We do know that there are three stages.

Stage 1: This can last up to 12 hours

☞ The muscles of the uterus begin to contract, resulting in the start of labour (birth).

☞ The baby is pushed down towards the opening at the base of the womb (cervix).

☞ The sac in which the baby has lived for the last nine months breaks (if it hasn't done so already) and the amniotic fluid flows away (water breaking).

☞ During this stage the neck of the womb is gradually opening.

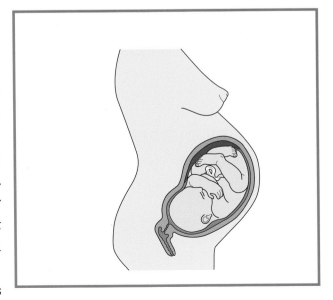

Stage 2: This can last from 20 minutes to an hour

☞ The neck of the womb opens (dilates) enough for the mother to push the baby through the birth canal.

☞ The end of this stage is marked by the birth of the baby.

☞ The umbilical cord, which has been the baby's lifeline, is clamped and cut.

☞ The baby cries and takes its first breath, which fills the lungs with air.

Stage 3: This can last between 5 minutes and an hour

☞ Even though the baby is born the contractions continue until the placenta is pushed out.

The journey of the last nine months has ended with the birth of the baby!

Healthy mother – healthy baby!

When you are old enough to have a baby, it is important to keep healthy during pregnancy. Here are some tips!

☞ Plan ahead!

☞ Before becoming pregnant take folic acid supplements. This reduces the chance of having a baby with spina bifida.

☞ Link in with the local health centre to organise antenatal care (care before birth).

☞ Eat a healthy, balanced diet.

☞ Avoid foods such as mould-ripened cheeses, raw eggs and foods made with unpasteurised milk. These may contain organisms that could result in food poisoning or miscarriage.

☞ Exercise regularly. This lifts your spirits and can help prevent depression.

☞ Avoid alcohol as it passes to the baby through the blood stream and can cause Foetal Alcohol Syndrome. This may result in the baby having learning difficulties.

☞ Never use illegal drugs. These can cause serious damage to the unborn baby.

☞ Do not smoke as it increases the risk of miscarriage or having a stillborn baby.

☞ Cut back on caffeine; this ensures that the baby will be a healthy weight.

Learning Log

Becoming a parent and giving birth to a baby bring huge responsibilities. Just because your body is physically ready for parenthood does not mean that you are ready psychologically (in your mind) or emotionally (feelings). Keep in mind the practical responsibilities of looking after a baby.

Write down some of the ways in which you are not yet ready for parenthood and why it is better to wait.

_____

_____

_____

_____

_____

▶▶ Peer pressure and other influences

Let's look at what 'peer pressure' means and how it can shape our picture of what it means to be male or female. We will also work out strategies for dealing with unhelpful peer pressure.

Gavin's Story

Gavin had spent a lot of time translating sentences into French for last night's homework. Just before class, his friends Rob and Jack said that they hadn't done it and they were going to tell the teacher it was too difficult.

'I got it done,' Gavin said lamely.

'Well, say you couldn't do it either or we'll get in trouble.'

When Ms Ferris asked if anybody had done the translation, Gavin stayed silent. He was furious that he had done all that work for nothing. Now, Ms Ferris would think that he couldn't do the exercise, but he knew that it wasn't worth it to go against the others.

Activity 3

Welcome to peer pressure!

1 What is peer pressure? In the space below, write all the words or phrases that you think of when you hear the words 'peer pressure'.

peer pressure

2 Write what you think peer pressure means.

_____

_____

Peer pressure

When you were young, your parents decided most things for you: what you ate, what you wore, where you went to school, who you played with. As you got older, you began to make your own decisions about these things.

In making these decisions, you are influenced by many factors: advertising, your parents and experiences, your friends, classmates and other people of your age (your peers).

Peer pressure happens when we do something we normally wouldn't do; or, because of the influence of people our age, we don't behave as we normally would.

All groups are affected by peer pressure. For example, adults buy four-wheel drive jeeps, even though they live in areas where these are unnecessary. And though they might disapprove, some adults give money for Communions and Confirmations because it is expected of them.

Peer pressure is not always a bad thing; in fact, it is often a good thing. We study harder if our friends take school seriously. We wash and keep clean because our friends expect us to. We have good manners because it is the norm in our group.

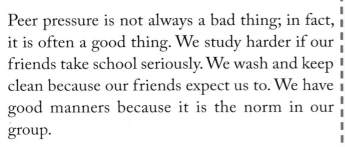

Some of the ways in which young people may be affected by peer pressure are:
- ☞ How hard they work at school
- ☞ The clothes they wear
- ☞ Who they hang around with
- ☞ Whether they drink or do drugs or not
- ☞ The decision to have a boy/girlfriend
- ☞ The way they speak, or their accent

However, sometimes we do things to fit in, although we know they are wrong, e.g. shoplifting, bullying and lying.

Peer pressure can come directly from others telling you what to do, or encouraging you, e.g. smoking a cigarette.

Peer pressure can come indirectly. This is when nothing is said, but you know what is expected (remember the Confirmation money).

Sometimes peer pressure comes from you. You might stop listening to a certain kind of music because you think your friends would laugh at you if they knew you liked it.

You have to be a strong person to do your own thing if it is different from what your peers do. In this way, peer pressure is linked to self-esteem. We will look at self-esteem in detail in the Emotional Health module.

How we are as males and females (our **sexuality**) is influenced by the expectations and comments of our friends. What we wear, our hobbies, our attitude to our families and our sexual behaviour are all influenced by what we believe others think of us.

Peer pressure and influences on sexuality

Below is a **lifeline** for a 14-year-old boy called Blake. It starts at birth and goes up to the present day. You will read that his attitude to his sexuality has been influenced by outside factors such as family structure and advertising, as well as peer pressure.

Blake's Lifeline

14 years: Bleaches tips of his hair blonde.

13 years: Chooses tech drawing instead of home economics for Junior Cert as his pals are doing it.

12 years: Uses Linx spray as the ads are cool.

10 years: Wears hoodies and track suit bottoms like his friends.

8 years: Supports Arsenal because his Dad does.

7 years: Gives up Irish Dancing because of teasing after school concert.

5 years: Older brothers tease him because he likes baking rice crispie buns with Mam.

3 years: Gets Lego, K'nex and transformers for Christmas.

1 year: All his baby clothes are blue.

0 years: The youngest of five boys with no sister.

Activity 4

1   Pick out the influences on Blake's role as a boy.

_____

_____

_____

2   In your opinion, were these influences positive or negative?

_____

_____

_____

3   Can you pick out one area of your life where your identity as a boy or girl was influenced by peer pressure?

_____

_____

_____

Activity 5

Dealing with peer pressure

A

You are in a shop and your friends steal some chocolate. They say, 'Now it's your turn'.

9

Your friends wear tiny skirts and tops when they go out. You are uncomfortable in these clothes. Your friends hassle you.

8

The people in your gang keep picking on a new boy because he looks different from them. They shout rude remarks at him. You don't want to be left out.

7

At the disco, your friends have a competition to see how many boys they can kiss in 20 minutes. You hate the idea.

6

You are staying with your friend. When you go out, she offers you some vodka. You don't want to drink it.

5

All your friends are playing soccer and you hate it. They tease you and call you a wimp.

4

You ride your bike to school and always wear a helmet. Your friends call you a 'Mammy's boy'.

3

Some classmates want to copy your work. You do not want to give it to them.

2

It's Christmas and your friends are asking for Nintendo Wii. Your parents can't afford it, but you don't want to be the only one without it.

When the teacher has assigned the cards, answer the following questions.

1. What could the young person on your card do to manage the peer pressure that he/she feels?

_____

_____

_____

Activity 5

2 Using your answers, put together an advice sheet for people of your age.

Managing Peer Pressure

_____
_____
_____
_____
_____
_____
_____
_____
_____
_____
_____
_____
_____
_____
_____
_____

Learning Log

1 One way in which I have been influenced by peer pressure is

_____

2 One way in which I exert peer pressure on others is

_____

▶▶ Managing relationships

As we get older, we form new and complex relationships. Generally, this is rewarding and fun, but it can sometimes cause problems. We will explore some of the relationships a second-year student might have. We will find out what is appropriate behaviour and what is unacceptable for different kinds of relationships.

Let's look at how you might begin a new relationship.

Establishing relationships

We have looked at the growing range of relationships you now have: parents, siblings, relatives, neighbours, school pals, classmates and cyber-friends. Over the next few years, you may have your first boyfriend or girlfriend. Many young people do not have a boyfriend or girlfriend until much later on and that's OK too.

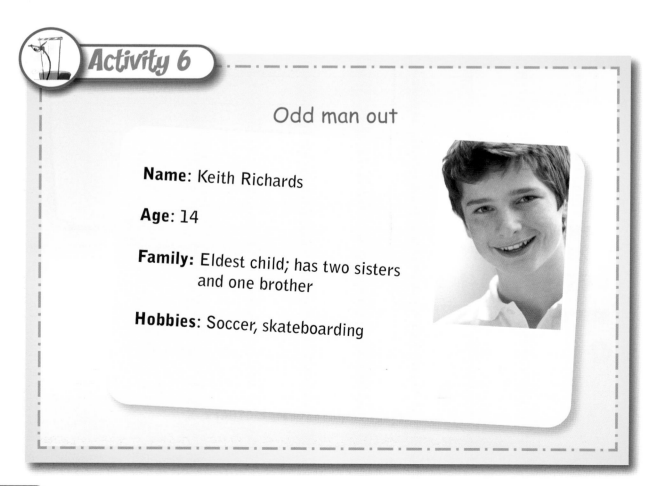

Activity 6

Odd man out

Name: Keith Richards

Age: 14

Family: Eldest child; has two sisters and one brother

Hobbies: Soccer, skateboarding

Activity 6

Most of Keith's friends go to the youth club disco every month. Keith has no real interest in girls, but he goes along for the laugh. Once there, his friends slag him because he isn't with someone. They tell several girls that he fancies them and wants to kiss them. Keith panics. He is happy just messing with the lads. But now he can see several girls pointing at him and laughing. He can't discuss this with his parents as he would be mortified.

1 What, do you think, should Keith do?

_____

_____

2 Why are Keith's friends acting this way?

_____

_____

3 How, do you think, might the girls be feeling?

_____

_____

4 What might be the result of the pressure Keith's friends are putting on him?

_____

_____

5 Is this an unusual situation?

_____

_____

Starting a relationship

1 Write in the empty speech bubble what the other person might say if he/she wanted to start a relationship.

Chicken curry – my favourite!

You have really improved since last term.

I'm getting soaked.

2 Fill in the Dos and Don'ts boxes of starting a relationship. After each piece of advice, write the reason for it. (One is done for you.)

Group Activity

Dos!

Don'ts!
Don't stalk the person (you'll scare him/her off!)

After listening to the Dos and Don'ts from the rest of the class, write the one you think is the best.

_____

Activity 8

Relationships – why bother?

Advantages	Disadvantages

1. On the left, above, write as many advantages as you can think of for having a boy/girlfriend.

2. On the right, above, write all the disadvantages of having a boy/girlfriend.

3. Add any new advantages and disadvantages that the rest of the class come up with.

Some young (and not so young!) people go from relationship to relationship. Others either wait for years to have their first relationship or have the same relationship for years. Each person is different.

What is important is that your relationships are positive and that you feel comfortable in them. Healthy relationships let you be yourself, help you to grow as an individual and make you feel good about yourself.

Learning Log

1 For me the most important factor in whether or not to have a boyfriend/girlfriend is

_____

2 I think that on a scale of 1 to 10 my ability to stand up to peer pressure is

_____

▶▶ Respecting myself and others

Different levels of relationships have different levels of behaviour that are right for them. How we behave in a relationship says something about how we respect ourselves and others. In the next activity, we will explore this.

Activity 9

Judy's day

Judy has breakfast with her family – father, sister, stepmother and stepbrother. Leaving the house, she almost knocks over the milkman in her rush for the bus. The bus driver waits for her and she flops down beside her best friend, Fred, whom she has known since second class.

Even though the school is having a half day all her teachers seem cross, including Auntie Claire who teaches Judy maths. The only fun Judy has is at break with her friends and at soccer practice even though coach is grumpy too.

After school, Judy has an appointment with the dentist to get her braces readjusted.

Then she buys a card for her Granny's birthday from Mrs Clancy in the corner shop and posts it at McCoy's post office. Gráinne McCoy sold her the stamp. She has been 'cool' with Judy since they stopped being best friends after they went to different secondary schools.

Activity 9

At 4 pm Judy has a music lesson with her mother's friend, Mr Wilson.

After tea, she puts her gear together for the scout hike next day. Fred's dad is the scout leader. Judy visits Owen's house and chats to his parents for a while before they go out. Owen and Judy have been going out for four weeks and usually go to the cinema on Friday night.

1 Reread Judy's day and see if you can find the different types of relationships that Judy has. These are divided into four categories:

☞ Family: immediate family and relatives
☞ Friends: close friends and others such as classmates, people she knows from the bus, etc.
☞ Professional: doctors, postman, school principal, etc.
☞ Intimate: wife, husband, partner, boyfriend/girlfriend, etc.

Circle the relationships in the story, using the following colours: blue for family, red for friends, green for professional and yellow for intimate relationships.

2 Write the relationships you find in the story, in the boxes below. The closer the relationship, the nearer the top of the list you are to put it. For example, Fred is Judy's best friend so his name will be at the top of the list. You can put the same person into more than one category.

Family	Friends	Professional	Intimate

3 Which relationships were easiest to categorise?

_____

_____

4 Which were the most difficult to decide on?

_____

_____

5 Were there any in more than one category?

_____

_____

_____

6 Do you find it believable that Fred is Judy's best friend? Explain your answer.

_____

_____

_____

7 Are there any categories that should never overlap? Explain your answer.

_____

_____

_____

_____

Appropriate relationships

There must be clear boundaries around relationships if they are to be safe and healthy. People who have a professional relationship with you, e.g. teachers, doctors, scout leaders and coaches, should never have an intimate relationship (physically or sexually close) with you. If that happens, or if you are uncomfortable or uneasy about any relationship, you should always talk to your parents or a trusted adult.

Judy's diary

Here is a piece from Judy's diary for this day.

> Friday 21st May
> '... really enjoyed soccer, got picked for the U-14 team.
> Excitement didn't last long – Mr Wilson is creepy. He keeps
> moving his chair closer and touching my leg. Today he stood
> behind me and leaned right down over me. I don't like it.
> I dread going next week but I can't tell Mom as she is a
> great friend of Mrs Wilson's. Anyway she would probably
> tell Dad and he might beat me again for causing trouble...'

In the space below write to Judy and give her some advice on what she could do. Try to be specific as to what actions she can take.

Dear Judy

1 What are the concerns that Judy has?

_____

_____

_____

2 From the answers the other students gave, is there anything else that Judy could do?

_____

_____

_____

IMPORTANT!

If you have any worries at all about what is going on in any of your relationships you should talk it over with your parents or another adult that you can trust. At school there are a number of people to talk to: the guidance counsellor, chaplain, class teacher, year head or indeed any staff member that you feel at ease with.

You can also get help with any worries you might have about what is OK in relationships by contacting any of the following organisations:

Childline Tel. 1800 66 66 66 www.childline.ie

The service is available 24 hours a day, 7 days a week, 365 days a year. Young people contact the service for many reasons such as bullying, sexuality, everyday chat and many other issues.

Samaritans Tel. 1850 60 90 90 email: jo@samaritans.org

Whatever you're going through, whether it's big or small, don't bottle it up. The Samaritans are there for you if you're worried about something, feel upset or confused, or just want to talk to someone. They offer a service by phone, email, letter and face-to-face in most of their branches.

CARI Tel. 1890 924567 email: helpline@cari.ie

The aim of the CARI Foundation is to provide a professional, child-centred therapy and counselling service to children, families, and groups who have been affected by child sexual abuse.

What is child sexual abuse?

Child sexual abuse is when someone involves a child or young person in sexual talk, touching or other activity. The child or young person might not fully understand what's happening, he/she may not know what to do and may find it scary or confusing.

What is physical abuse?

Physical abuse occurs when a child is deliberately injured or is injured due to the deliberate failure of the child's parent or guardian to protect the child. If you are being physically abused you should tell an adult, maybe a family member or a teacher. You could phone the Gardaí (just dial 999) or Childline. The number is above.

Remember! No adult can promise confidentiality if there is risk to any child.

Learning Log

1 Something positive about my relationships:

_____

2 If I were worried about myself or a friend's relationship I would

_____

_____

_____

Recognising and expressing feelings and emotions

Love is one of the most discussed aspects of life. From 'Love hurts' to 'Love makes the world go round', opinions on love differ. Let's examine what love means to us.

 **Activity 11**

What is love?

1 On this page put words, colours, phrases, pictures or symbols that represent love or people showing love.

What is love?

2 Talk to other students about their collages. How are they different from yours? Are there any similarities?

Group Activity

Activity 12

Corinthians 13:4

Love is patient and kind. Love is not jealous or boastful or proud or rude. It does not demand its own way. It is not irritable, and it keeps no record of being wronged. It does not rejoice about injustice but rejoices whenever the truth wins out. Love never gives up, never loses faith, is always hopeful, and endures through every circumstance.

I Wanna Be Yours

I wanna be your vacuum cleaner
breathing in your dust
I wanna be your Ford Cortina
I will never rust
If you like your coffee hot
let me be your coffee pot
You call the shots
I wanna be yours

I wanna be your raincoat
for those frequent rainy days
I wanna be your dreamboat
when you want to sail away
Let me be your teddy bear
take me with you anywhere
I don't care
I wanna be yours

I wanna be your electric meter
I will not run out
I wanna be the electric heater
you'll get cold without

I wanna be your setting lotion
hold your hair in deep devotion
Deep as the deep Atlantic ocean
that's how deep is my devotion

John Cooper Clarke

The Rose

Some say love, it is a river
That drowns the tender reed
Some say love, it is a razor
That leaves your soul to bleed
Some say love, it is a hunger
An endless aching need
I say love, it is a flower
And you, its only seed

It's the heart, afraid of breaking
That never learns to dance
It's the dream, afraid of waking
That never takes the chance
It's the one who won't be taken
Who cannot seem to give
And the soul, afraid of dying
That never learns to live

Amanda McBroom

Read the three pieces above and pick out the line or phrase you think best explains what love means.

The line/phrase/word I chose is

_____

I picked this line/phrase/word because

_____

Write a 'Love is ...' poem or draw a cartoon based on your answers to the questions in Activity 12. You can do this on your own or with others.

Love is ...

Learning Log

I think being loved and loving someone is important because

_____

_____

_____

_____

☆ Module Review

Module _____

In this module I learned about

_____

I think that this will help me _____

_____

I liked _____

_____

I did not like _____

_____

I would like to learn more about _____

_____

This topic links with (another topic or SPHE module, or

another subject) _____

_____

MODULE 1

Emotional Health

Introduction

Many factors contribute to our emotional health and wellbeing. In year 1, you learned how to recognise and express your feelings. You learned also to respect the feelings of others. Feeling good about ourselves and helping others to feel good about themselves are essential ingredients in our emotional health. Let's explore this in more detail.

The topics in this module are:

▸▸ Self-confidence

▸▸ Body image

 ## Self-confidence

What makes you feel good about yourself? You may have heard the words self-esteem and self-confidence before, but do you know what they mean? Why are they important? How can you build up your self-esteem and self-confidence?

What is self-esteem?

The word 'esteem' has to do with how much you value something. So, 'self-esteem' has to do with how much you value yourself; how worthwhile and capable you feel.

People with healthy levels of self-esteem have a realistic view of themselves. They see themselves as liked. They accept their weaknesses and celebrate their good qualities without thinking they're better than other people.

What is self-confidence?

Self-confidence is related to self-esteem, but it's a little bit different. Self-confidence is a belief in yourself and in your ability to do something well. It is especially important when facing new challenges and new situations.

Building self-confidence is an important part of succeeding. For example, sports people use psychologists to help them boost their confidence and self-belief.

 Activity 1

'Me' collage

1 Make a collage using pictures, colours, drawings or words as symbols of the following statements about you. Spend a few minutes thinking about this before you start. Keep this collage as part of your SPHE portfolio.

> ☞ One thing I like about my body
> ☞ One thing I like about my family
> ☞ One thing I like about my personality
> ☞ One aim/ambition I have
> ☞ One hobby/interest I have
> ☞ One thing I would like to change about myself

Group Activity

2 Discuss your collage with other students. Talk about some of the things you have put in it.

3 Finish the following sentences and remember to explain your answers.

(a) The part I found easiest about this activity was

_____

_____

(b) The part I found most difficult about this exercise was

_____

_____

(c) I found talking to my classmates about the collage was

_____

_____

Building block of self-esteem

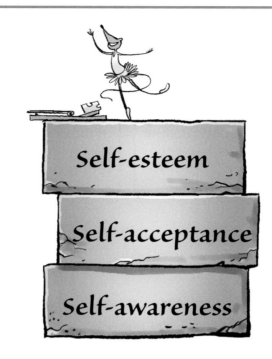

Self-esteem

Self-acceptance

Self-awareness

Part of building up self-esteem is working on your knowledge and understanding of yourself (**self-awareness**) and liking yourself as you are (**self-acceptance**).

It is normal to try to improve yourself, but some aspects are difficult to change. For example, if you are bad at sports and accept that you will never make the school basketball team and concentrate instead on what you are good at, then your self-esteem is likely to be strong.

Unfortunately, we find it easier to focus on our shortcomings and probably find exercises like Activity 1 difficult.

Promoting a sense of wellbeing in others

Activity 2

1. Complete the brainstorm by writing in the ways people make others feel good about themselves.

How do we make others feel good about themselves?

2. Discuss your brainstorm in class and add in any ideas that other students may have had. Draw a circle around the one that is your favourite.

Class Activity

Giving and receiving compliments

One way of making people feel good about themselves is to compliment them.

A **compliment** is an expression of praise or admiration, either in words or by an action.

Giving a compliment is a two-way process. It makes both people feel good about themselves. Some people feel uncomfortable when they get a compliment and instead of saying 'thanks' they try to brush it off by saying something negative. Remember that part of the skill of being assertive is being able to give and receive compliments.

Compliments

1 Get into groups of six. Write your name on the gift box. Pass your workbook to the person on your right and take the workbook of the student on your left. In one of the balloons write a positive thing about the student whose name is on the box. Keep passing on the workbooks and writing positive things until you get your book back.

2 When others were writing good things about me, I felt

_____

_____

3 When I was writing compliments about others, I felt

_____

_____

Learning Log

Read all the compliments written about you in Activity 3 and write the one you liked best on the line below. (Remember many people feel embarrassed writing good things about themselves!) When your turn comes to read your compliment for the class start the sentence with the words 'I am ...'.

The compliment about me that I liked best is

_____

Body image

Body image is a term for how a person sees his or her body. It has two aspects: how you think your body looks and how you feel about it. For example, somebody might think his/her body doesn't look great, but might feel fine about it because of being good at music. Another person might think his/her body is not great and be upset about it. That person might avoid going out and wear baggy clothes to cover up.

Can you see how your self-esteem can affect your body image and how your body image can affect your self-esteem?

The notion of the ideal body has changed over time. For generations curves were seen as a sign of health and money. Marilyn Monroe is reported to have been size 14. The 'super-skinny' look is a recent fad driven by the fashion industry.

107

Sometimes we think that body image is an issue for girls only, but that is not true. There is just as much pressure on boys to fit into what is considered an acceptable body shape.

As young people go through adolescence (and sometimes earlier) they can become concerned about how their body is growing and changing. *SPHE 1* looked at this and told us that there is no set time frame for these changes. Because adolescence marks the beginning of you becoming independent of your parents and making your own friends, there can be anxiety about fitting in and being accepted. You may compare yourself with people on TV, or in magazines, music videos and films. Classmates and peers may make hurtful remarks about your shape or others' body shape.

Sometimes, parents can criticise their children's looks or physical abilities without thinking of the effect this can have on the body image and self-esteem of young people.

The diet industry

The diet industry (foods, programmes and drugs) is huge. It is estimated that in the USA alone between $40 billion and $100 billion is spent on diets each year. This is more than the combined budget for education, welfare and health. Pictures of impossibly thin people keep this industry going, as they create a notion of beauty that is unattainable.

Know your body shape

☞ **Rectangle or tower shape**

Fat is distributed equally over the body, and the chest and hips are the same size. This is the typical 'adolescent boy' shape. This shape is seen in both men and women.

☞ **Pear shape**

Fat is stored in the hips and legs. This is more common in women than in men.

☞ **Apple shape**

Most weight is found in the top half of the body and is called 'busty' in women. The most common place that men carry their weight is in their 'beer belly', which for health reasons is also the most dangerous place for men.

☞ **Hourglass shape**

The 'Barbie' shape; only seen in women.

Activity 4

Advertising and body image

When women talk clothes . . .

they talk of the beauty of *Celanese* Fabrics

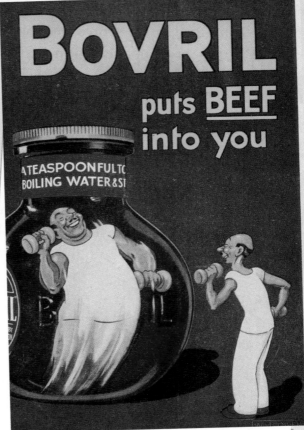

BOVRIL puts **BEEF** into you

A TEASPOONFUL TO BOILING WATER & ST...

1 What messages do these advertisements give you about body image?

_____

_____

_____

_____

2 To what extent do these pictures represent people in ordinary life?

_____

_____

_____

_____

Learning Log

Make out a **realistic** advertisement for (a) one of the products or services shown in Activity 4, or (b) a product for which the advertising industry targets young people today.

Keep the advertisement you create in your SPHE portfolio.

☆ Module Review

Module _____

In this module I learned about

_____

I think that this will help me _____

_____

I liked _____

_____

I did not like _____

_____

I would like to learn more about _____

_____

This topic links with (another topic or SPHE module, or

another subject) _____

_____

MODULE 8
Influences and Decisions

Introduction

Making decisions is something you do every day. Understanding what influences you in making decisions is not something you think about too often. In this module, we will look at how we influence other people and how others influence us, both positively and negatively. We will also explore ways in which we make decisions and learn how to make a good decision.

The topics in this module are:

» Positive and negative influences

» Making decisions

 ## Positive and negative influences

In making a decision, we are often influenced by people or events. Influences may be positive or negative.

Positive influences are ones that affect our lives for the better.

Negative influences are those that affect our lives in a way that is not in our best interest.

Activity 1

A tough decision!

Here is an imaginary situation! A boat is coming back from a daytrip to an offshore island when a storm blows up. There are eight people on board. Despite their best efforts, the boat begins to sink. A boat nearby sees them in difficulty and offers to take some people on board. You are on this boat and you can take only four of the eight from the sinking boat. You must decide, quickly, who to take on board and why.

Here are the eight:

1 Paddy is 19 years old. He has a history of crime and a prison record.

2 Mick is a doctor. He is an alcoholic and has a young family.

3 Jenny is 57 years old. She set up a shelter for homeless people in her town.

4 Kate is the mother of four young children.

5 Jack is a research scientist who leads a team working on a cure for cancer.

6 Meg is 14 years old. She was involved in a car accident when she was six and is now disabled.

7 Ray is 27 years old. He is an international soccer star.

8 Susan is 24 years old. She is HIV positive and has twin sons at home.

Activity 1

1 Answer the questions in the box below. Remember you must choose four people.

Who will you take on board?	Why did you decide on this person?

2 When you have decided and recorded your reasons work with others and try to come to a group agreement about who you will take on board. Record your group's final four here:

Group Activity

Who will you take on board?	Why did you decide on this person?

3 If some of those you chose on your own were not included in the final four, what influenced you to change your mind?
☞ Pressure from others
☞ A good reason that you had not thought of
☞ You just decided to go with the flow
☞ You wanted to avoid an argument
☞ You decided to wait and see what others thought

4 Do you think you influenced people in making the final choice? If so, how?

_____

_____

Learning Log

1 Answer (a) or (b).

(a) I enjoyed this activity because

_____

(b) I did not enjoy this activity because

_____

2 One thing I learned about how I influence others is

_____

3 One thing I learned about how I am influenced by others is

_____

 ## Activity 2

Let's look at some everyday decisions and how you might be influenced in making them. Then say whether these were positive or negative influences.

Think of three decisions you made recently and fill in the table below. Two examples are given.

Decision	Influences	Reason for decision
1 Clothes I bought	Friends, fashion	I looked well
2 To smoke or not	Friends	I wanted to fit in
3		
4		
5		

Activity 2

☞ The positive influences were

_____

_____

☞ The negative influences were

_____

_____

☞ To minimise the negative influences in my life I will

_____

_____

☞ To maximise the positive influences I will

_____

_____

Activity 3

How I influence others

1 Think about the ways in which you influence other people. These could be your friends, sisters and brothers, peers in school or others.

2 (a) Write down four ways in which you influence others – two positive and two negative influences.

(b) Then see how you can turn one of the negative influences around to make it positive and record this also (e.g. I often use bad language at home and now I notice my young sister doing the same. I will watch my language in future).

	Positive	Negative
(a) 1		
(a) 2		
(b)		

Learning Log

1. Something new I learned about the way I influence others is

_____

_____

2. One thing I learned about how I am influenced by others is

_____

_____

▶▶ Making decisions

Learning how to make decisions is a key life skill. There will be times when the decisions that you make may not be the correct ones at the time and you can learn from this too. Remember practice makes perfect!

 Activity 4

Kevin's decision

Kevin had known for some time that things were not good between his mother and father, so it was with some relief that he learned that they were going to separate. Kevin's two younger sisters were going to live with their mother, but would still see their dad every week. As Kevin was now 14 years old, his parents asked him to decide where he wanted to live. Kevin has a decision to make.

Put yourself in Kevin's shoes and describe, in the space below, how you would go about making this decision. Then say what your decision was and why this was your decision.

How I would go about making this decision:

_____

_____

_____

_____

_____

_____

I decided to _____ because

_____

_____

How to make decisions

Here are six different ways (styles) that people use to make decisions:

☞ 'Weigh up pros and cons'
☞ Allow others to influence you
☞ Play safe and take least risky option
☞ Go with your gut and opt for what feels best
☞ Ask for advice
☞ Do nothing; adopt a 'wait and see' approach

Now that you know the different ways in which people make decisions, see which one you used in making your decision about Kevin in Activity 4.

Alcohol debate

In groups of three the whole class prepares a debate on the topic 'Alcohol should be banned'. Use the information from the last activity.

Your teacher will tell you whether you are for or against the statement (motion).

Method

☞ Each team will have three speakers: first, second and last speaker.

☞ Each speaker talks for a minimum of 90 seconds and a maximum of 120 seconds (2 minutes).

☞ Decide what your points or arguments are going to be and share them.

☞ The first speakers on the teams introduce the topic and explain what it means. They also give an outline of what each team member will say and then make a point or two of their own.

☞ The second speakers develop their points and also argue against the points of the opposition.

☞ The last speakers make one major point, dismiss the arguments of the opposition and sum up their teams' case.

☞ One group for the motion and one group against the motion will be chosen to debate in front of the class. The audience will mark each speaker, using the marking scheme below.

Score sheet for debate

Team name: **Total team score:**

Speaker	Content (50)	Presentation (30)	Cross comment* (20)	Total
1				
2				
3				

*Cross comment means how the speaker attacks what members of the opposite team said and defends what earlier speakers on their side already said.

Team name: **Total team score:**

Speaker	Content (50)	Presentation (30)	Cross comment* (20)	Total
1				
2				
3				

Cannabis and its effects

Cannabis can cause both depression and euphoria (excitement, exhilaration). These effects can be due to the strength of the cannabis, the length of time it has been stored, the amount used and the way it is taken.

Cannabis is also called hash, pot, weed, ganja, hemp, grass, dope, shake and jungle juice. A cannabis cigarette may be called a joint, a reefer or a spliff.

Herbal cannabis

Herbal cannabis is the dried leaves and flower head of the cannabis plant. It looks like dried herbs and is smoked in a cigarette. This may be called marijuana, grass, ganja, pot, weed or skunk.

Cannabis resin

Cannabis resin is widely known as hashish or hash. This is a green/brown block or slab of resin and is the most common type of cannabis found in Ireland. This can be heated and smoked in a pipe or bong, or mixed with tobacco in a cigarette.

Cannabis oil

Hashish oil, more commonly called hash oil, is a thick liquid made from dissolving hashish or marijuana in solvents like acetone, alcohol, butane, or petroleum ether.

Cannabis contains over 400 different chemicals including THC which causes euphoria and CBD which is a depressant.

Using cannabis

☞ Increases heart rate and lowers blood pressure and this is risky for people with heart disease.

☞ Interferes with short-term memory and learning abilities; even simple maths ability can be affected for up to 24 hours.

☞ Interferes with motor coordination and the ability to drive.

☞ Can cause mental/emotional effects such as confusion, severe panic and anxiety.

Long-term effects of using cannabis

If you use cannabis often and over a long period, it can damage your health.

☞ The effects include loss of memory, difficulty concentrating and being easily distracted.

☞ Cannabis produces the same harmful effects as tobacco (see *SPHE 1*) including chronic bronchitis, lung damage and cancer.

☞ People with a family history of mental illness are particularly at risk from cannabis use. It can trigger schizophrenia (bi-polar disorder) or depression in vulnerable individuals.

☞ It causes fertility problems in both men and women.

☞ Research shows that young people who use cannabis regularly are more likely to drop out of school.

☞ Cannabis is just as dangerous for babies in the womb as tobacco smoke. After birth it can reach the baby through breast milk.

Caution!

Using cannabis brings a young person into the criminal world of drug dealers and gangland crime. This market is controlled by criminals and the money from drugs goes into their pockets.

Did You Know?

It is illegal to grow, produce, supply or possess cannabis. It is also an offence to allow premises to be used for cultivating, supplying or smoking cannabis.

Under current legislation, if you have a conviction for using cannabis you will have a permanent criminal record. This can be a serious problem if you want to apply for certain jobs in state or other organisations, or get a Garda clearance for foreign travel/work visas.

?

A person can be found guilty of 'supplying' drugs even if he/she did not get money for them.

People with a drug conviction will be refused visas for the USA.

 **Activity 5**

Cloze test

Using the information you have learned about cannabis see how much of this cloze test you can fill in.

Cannabis comes in three forms: _____, _____ and _____.
Cannabis is usually taken by _____. Cannabis does not fit into any one category of drugs as it is a sedative but also can cause _____.
It has many slang names including g _____ , h _____ , w _____ and d _____. It has over _____ chemicals in it. Possession, use and supply of cannabis are _____.
Memory loss and severe panic attacks can be _____ - _____ effects of using it. H _____ effects can include lung damage, increased risk of d _____ and s _____ in some people, and a decrease in male and female _____.

Learning Log

One thing that I learned about cannabis that surprised me is

_____

 ## Cannabis: why, why not?

In this topic we will learn that cannabis use affects not only the person using it. It has an influence on the user's friends, family, community and society in general.

 **Activity 6**

Risky business

1 Write in the box below what you think the word 'risk' means.

Risk means

2 Write a list of the risks in using alcohol (see *SPHE 1* pages 126–127) and cannabis. You might consider health, society, family, the law, money, education, etc.

Alcohol risks	Cannabis risks

Activity 6

3 Add any other risks that you did not think of, but the other groups did, onto the end of your list.

4 Does cannabis and alcohol use have an effect on people outside those who use them? List those people here:

_____

_____

_____

_____

_____

Activity 7

Storyboard

Using what you have learned in Activity 6, complete the last four frames in the storyboard overleaf. Before you start, think about what you want to draw.

Group Activity

The story should make it clear what risks were taken and how they affected different people.

Learning Log

After looking at the storyboards of the other groups in your class finish the following sentences:

1 Alcohol and cannabis use can affect young people on a personal level in the following ways:

_____

_____

2 Alcohol and cannabis use can affect young people on a social level in the following ways:

_____

_____

☆ Module Review

Module _____

In this module I learned about

_____

I think that this will help me_____

_____

I liked_____

_____

I did not like_____

_____

I would like to learn more about_____

_____

This topic links with (another topic or SPHE module, or

another subject)_____

_____

MODULE 10

Personal Safety

Introduction

Knowing how to keep safe is an important part of becoming independent. Last year, in *SPHE 1*, we explored the topics of fire safety, accident prevention in school, road safety and keeping safe when you are out. This year we will explore the issues of safety in the home, safety on the farm and water safety. We will also look at cyber safety (e.g. mobile phone and the Internet).

The topics in this module are:

» Accidents in the home
» Farm safety
» Water safety
» Cyber safety

 ## Accidents in the home

We are all aware that accidents can and do happen. Accidents are more likely to happen in the home than anywhere else! Let's have a look at the different hazards that can be found in the home.

Remember!
A hazard is anything that increases the risk of having an accident.

Hazards

There are three generations of people living in a house.

☞ An elderly granny
☞ A mother
☞ A father
☞ Their two children aged fifteen years and one year

1 On the next page, study the different rooms in the house and identify possible hazards in each room.

2 Circle the hazard in red.

Remember to think of the different people living in the house!

3 Then summarise the hazards on page 141.

> **Remember!**
> Different hazards pose different risks to different people and in different places.

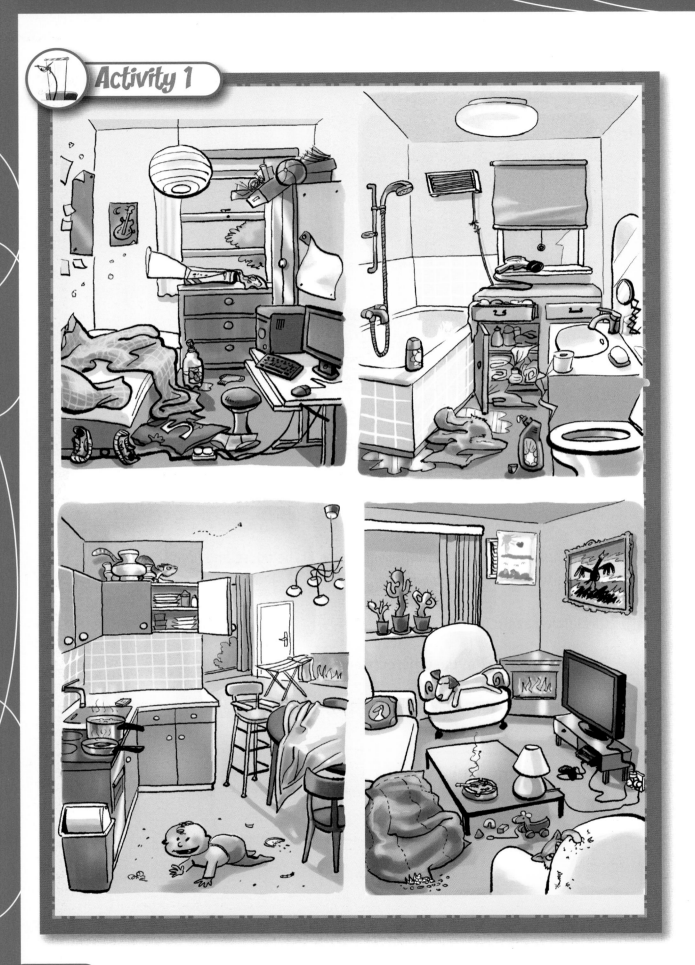

Hazards in a teenager's bedroom

1 _____

2 _____

3 _____

4 _____

5 _____

6 _____

Hazards in a bathroom

1 _____

2 _____

3 _____

4 _____

5 _____

6 _____

Hazards in a kitchen/diner

1 _____

2 _____

3 _____

4 _____

5 _____

6 _____

Hazards in a TV room

1 _____

2 _____

3 _____

4 _____

5 _____

6 _____

Now that you know a lot more about hazards in the home, work with other students to design a poster outlining tips for safety in the home.

Making the home a safer place for all

Learning Log

I can contribute to making my home a safer place by

_____

_____

▶▶ Farm safety

This summer, for a change, instead of going to the seaside for holidays you have been invited to stay with your cousins on their farm in the country. You were there when you were younger and are excited about returning! You also know that in Ireland an average of twenty people die in farm accidents each year. Thousands more are injured. All these accidents are preventable. Let's look at farm safety.

The following things could all be potential hazards on a farm

☞ Machinery

☞ Animals

☞ Electricity, e.g. power lines

☞ Chemicals, e.g. fuels, fertilisers and weed killers

☞ Water, e.g. water tanks, waste water, abandoned water well

☞ Storage of grain

☞ Farm equipment, e.g. ladders, tyres and forks

☞ People dressed in clothes that could catch, e.g. long coats

☞ Smoking near fuel

Activity 3

Here is a picture of a farm and its surroundings showing some possible hazards. With another student see how many hazards you can spot. Mark each one with a red triangle and say why you think it is a hazard. Then write some tips for young people of your age, alerting them to the ways of keeping safe on the farm.

Be Alert! Be Aware! Stay Alive!

_____

_____

_____

_____

_____

Learning Log

All farms are required to have an up-to-date Safety Statement. Find out what this means and describe it briefly in the space below.

A Farm Safety Satement is

_____

_____

_____

_____

▶▶ Water safety

Now that summer holidays are approaching perhaps you will spend time at the beach, swimming and having fun. The Irish Water Safety Association tells us that, on average, 160 people drown every year in Ireland. Many of these drownings happen while people are enjoying themselves by the sea and all are preventable.

Let's see how much you know about swimming safely. Look at Activity 4 on the next page and test your knowledge of swimming safety.

Remember!

You may not live or holiday near a beach but don't forget there are safety rules for swimming in rivers, canals and lakes too. There are tips from the Irish Water Safety Association for safe swimming in these places. Look at their website for more tips for safe swimming: *www.iws.ie*.

Safe swimming

There are messages about safe swimming in each of the cartoons opposite. See if you can match the statements below with the cartoons on the opposite page. The messages are jumbled!

1 Don't swim alone

Someone with you could help, or go to get help, if you got into difficulty. He/she would also know more details if you were to have an accident, e.g. last place sighted, details of injuries, etc.

2 Don't swim just after eating

Wait at least one hour after eating before going swimming. This will give your body a chance to digest the food and minimise the risk of a swimmer suffering a cramp or a stitch.

3 Don't swim when you're hot or tired

Your body is less able to cope with extreme coldness when you're hot or tired and your body temperature may drop suddenly, giving rise to shock or hypothermia.

4 Don't swim in strange places

You may not be aware of the dangers, such as currents, tides, riptides, marine life and submerged objects.

5 Don't swim out after anything drifting

The object may look closer than it is. You will have to swim the same length back to shore.

6 Don't stay in the water too long

Coldness will impair your judgement and you may develop hypothermia.

7 Swim parallel and close to the shore

You are in sight of shore if you get tired, someone can help and you can walk back to shore when you're finished.

8 Never use air mattresses

They can be picked up by the wind and blown out to sea. They can also drift out to sea.

9 Pay attention to signs on the beach

They can include warning signs, e.g. rocks, and can potentially keep you away from dangerous situations.

10 Learn to use equipment before trying it out

This is to ensure you are competent in its use and won't get into difficulty easily in the water.

Activity 4

A

B

C

D

E

F

G

H

I

J

© Irish Water Safety Association

Learning Log

Think about the place where you swim and write down three things that you will be more aware of when next you go swimming.

1. _____
2. _____
3. _____

▶▶ Cyber safety

Cyberspace has been compared to a big city with different routes into it, e.g. mobile phones, Internet and games machines. These are all different forms of Information and Communications Technology (ICT). As with all big cities it is important to know how to keep yourself safe as you travel through the different parts. These activities will help you stay safe in this city of 'Cyberspace'.

 Activity 5

Let's look at how you or your family have used mobile phones, the Internet or games consoles (ICT). What were they used for? Brainstorm these and write them in the brainstorm bubble on page 149.

Activity 5

ICT

Remember!
These are useful tools, but can be open to abuse and need to be handled with care.

Activity 6

How much do you know?

1 See if you can match these terms with their definitions. The first one is done for you.

Terms
WWW   AUP   Netiquette   Blog   Web log   IM   Chat room
Cyberbullying   Flame   Bebo   Facebook   Twitter   Profile

Computers around the world linked together

World Wide Web (www)

Activity 6

Terms

AUP   Netiquette   Blog   Web log   IM   Chat room
Cyberbullying   Flame   Bebo   Facebook   Twitter   Profile

A set of written rules in an organisation, outlining what users are not allowed to do when using computers (or any other form of IT).

_____

Etiquette on the Internet. Using the Internet in a way that respects your own and others' privacy. This applies especially to how you communicate with others through email and chat rooms.

_____

Way of communicating online, individually, or with one or more people. You have a one-to-one conversation with each person separately. Messages are sent in text.

_____

Bullying carried out through the Internet, a mobile phone or any other form of ICT.

_____

A personal online diary or journal that you can post updates to regularly and can be read by the others who know you have set up such a site.

_____

A site on the Internet where people can communicate in 'real time'. Messages typed by the users develop into an ongoing conversation. Each person is aware of what you are saying to others.

_____

Deliberately posting comments or messages on an online discussion site with the intention of insulting or hurting others.

_____

Activity 6

Social networking sites that enable friends to communicate and share information through IM and email. When registered with the site you have your own personal homepage, which you access through your own password.

_____

Information about yourself that you place on your social networking homepage. This is information you wish others to know, e.g. your hobbies, interests, likes and dislikes.

_____

2 Here are some more words associated with ICT. Find out what they mean and write in the definitions.

(MMS)

_____

_____

Skype

_____

_____

Spam

_____

_____

YouTube

_____

_____

Phishing

_____

_____

Newsgroups and bulletin boards

_____

_____

Safe surfing

Here are some rules for 'safe surfing'. These rules apply to mobile phones as well as to computers.

Rules for safe surfing

☞ Be careful when using your mobile phone. Use it to talk only to people you know.

☞ Never disclose your password to others online.

☞ Keep yourself as anonymous as possible online. Never disclose personal information.

☞ Be careful about any photographs that you post. Your profile on a social networking site is in public space.

☞ Your screen name should not allow others to identify who you are.

☞ Only post what you are happy with others seeing and knowing about you. Once you post information you cannot take it back and others can save it on their computers.

☞ Think about setting up a private chat room for you and your friends. Invite only those who you want to be part of the chat room to join.

☞ Never arrange to meet a new online friend in person. People may not be who they say they are.

☞ In a chat room do not use your screen name. Use a nickname instead.

☞ Never involve yourself in flaming or cyberbullying.

☞ Trust your instincts! If you are suspicious of anything while online, or if you are threatened or are uncomfortable, exit from the site immediately and tell a trusted adult.

☞ Inform the Gardaí if you think it best to do so. Doing so may not only protect you but may protect others in the future.

Activity 7

Now that you have read the rules for safe surfing, decide what advice you would give to the young people in the scenarios below.

Maya has been talking online to Trish for some time. Maya has given Trish her mobile number and a photo. Now Trish wants to meet Maya in town.

What should Maya do? Why? Why not?

_____

_____

_____

Jack is talking to a friend online when he gets a message saying that he has a problem with his computer. He is asked to type in his online password immediately.

Should Jack do this? Why? Why not?

_____

_____

_____

Jill gets anonymous text messages on her mobile phone at night. The messages are upsetting. Last night Jill found the same messages on her Bebo site.

What could or should Jill do?

_____

_____

_____

Unknown to his parents, Alan bought some DVDs from an Internet site, using his mother's credit card. When the statement came there were many items on it that she had not bought. At the same time, she started to receive spam messages on email, making all sorts of offers. Questions are being asked!

What should Alan do now?

_____

_____

What should Alan have learned from this?

_____

_____

Learning Log

1 Using my mobile phone I need to be careful about
_____

2 One thing that is great about the Internet is
_____

3 Something that I need to be careful of when I am online is
_____

4 If I run into a difficulty while online I can
_____

☆ Module Review

Module _____

In this module I learned about

_____

I think that this will help me_____

_____

I liked_____

_____

I did not like_____

_____

I would like to learn more about_____

_____

This topic links with (another topic or SPHE module, or
another subject)_____

_____

Congratulations!

You have completed your second year in secondary school. Hopefully you have had a good year, and your experiences have helped you to become more confident and prepared for the challenges in the third year.

Let's have a look back over your second year!

Do a stick drawing of yourself in the middle of the page below and around it write some of your thoughts about your year. Use the hints to help you.

IN SEPTEMBER
How I felt starting second year
_____
_____

One thing that I loved about second year
_____
_____

A good experience that I had
_____
_____

A challenge that I managed well
_____
_____

A disappointment that I had
_____
_____

Someone who helped me
_____

A new skill that I learned
_____